MANITOBA STUDIES IN NATIVE HISTORY

Manitoba Studies in Native History publishes new scholarly interpretations of the historical experience of native peoples in the western interior of North America. The series is under the editorial direction of a board representative of the scholarly and native communities of Manitoba.

UNIVERSITY OF WINNIPEG, 515 Portage Ave. Winnipeg, MB R3B 2E9 Canada

MANITOBA STUDIES IN NATIVE HISTORY IV

The Plains Cree: Trade, Diplomacy and War, 1790 to 1870

JOHN S. MILLOY

THE UNIVERSITY OF MANITOBA PRESS

© The University of Manitoba Press 1988
Winnipeg, Manitoba R3T 2N2
Printed in Canada
Reprinted with corrections 1990

Design: Norman Schmidt

Frontispiece: Cree Indian camp at the Elbow of the Saskatchewan River, 1871 (National Archives of Canada, neg. T-354 [H-703])

Cover illustration: Paul Kane painting of a Cree from Fort Pitt (*"Kee-a-kee-ka-sa-coo-way,"* or "The Man that Gives the War Whoop"), courtesy of the Royal Ontario Museum, Toronto, Canada [ROM #912.1.42]

Cataloguing in Publication Data

Milloy, John Sheridan
The Plains Cree
(Manitoba studies in native history, ISSN 0826-9416 ; 4)
Includes bibliographical footnotes and index.
ISBN 0-88755-141-6 (bound) – ISBN 0-88755-623-X (pbk.)

1. Cree Indians - History. 2. Cree Indians - Commerce -
History. 3. Cree Indians - Wars - History. 4. Indians
of North America - Northwest, Canadian - History.
I. Title. II Series.

E99.C88M54 1988   971.2'0000497   C88-098099-0

This series is published with the financial support of the people of Manitoba, the Honourable Bonnie Mitchelson, Minister of Culture, Heritage and Recreation. The publication of this volume was also assisted by a grant from the Canada Council.

Manitoba Studies in Native History Board of Directors: J. Burelle, J. Fontaine, G. Friesen, E. Harper, E. LaRocque, R. McKay, W. Moodie, G. Schultz, D. Young.

Contents

Contents continued

Note On Synonyms

The names given to plains tribes differ not only within a specific primary source and between sources, but they also change over the period of the fur trade. The following is a list of tribes, including the most common names and their synonyms.

1 Plains Cree: Nehethawa (and variations of this spelling), Cristineaux and Knisteneaux, Southerd, Southern and Cris.

2 Assiniboine: numerous variations of this spelling, and sometimes with the addition of "poet," and Stoney (also used to refer to Wood or Mountain Assiniboine).

3 Blackfoot "Confederacy": Archithi (or Archithe), Archithnie (it is not clear whether this title was meant to apply to the whole Confederacy or just the Blackfoot tribe proper), Slave Indians and Plains Tribes.

4 Blackfoot: Siksika and Blackfoot proper.

5 Piegan: a member tribe of the Blackfoot Confederacy sometimes referred to as Muddy River Indians.

6 Blood: a member tribe of the Blackfoot Confederacy constantly referred to by that title.

7 Sarcee: this tribe is a subdivision of the Beaver Indians. The Sarcee joined the Confederacy in the second half of the eighteenth century. Known also as Circer, Sussee and Sacree, and variations on these.

8 Gros Ventre: a sometime ally of the Confederacy referred to as Naywattame Poets, Atsina (anthropological designation), Gros Ventre des Prairies, Big Belly, Fall and Rapid Indians.

9 Sioux: Naudawisses and variations of this spelling.

10 Crow: Gens des Corbeaus (sic), Crow and Rocky Mountain Crow.

11 Snake: Gens du Serpent and Shoshoni.

12 Cheyenne: Schaines.

13 Hidatsa: Gros Ventre, Big Belly and Minnetaree. The confusion between these tribes and the Atsina (8 above) is minimized by the totally different ways of life of these two tribes.

14 Arapaho: Tattooed.

15 Mandan: this is the standard title.

16 Arikaras: there are numerous variations of this spelling (Arikarees) and Rees.

17 Kootenay: Cooteney, Koutenai and Cuttencha.

18 Ojibwa: Chippewa and Ojibway (there are many variations of this spelling) Saulteaux, Saulteurs, Bungee.

19 Flathead: Salish.

Tables

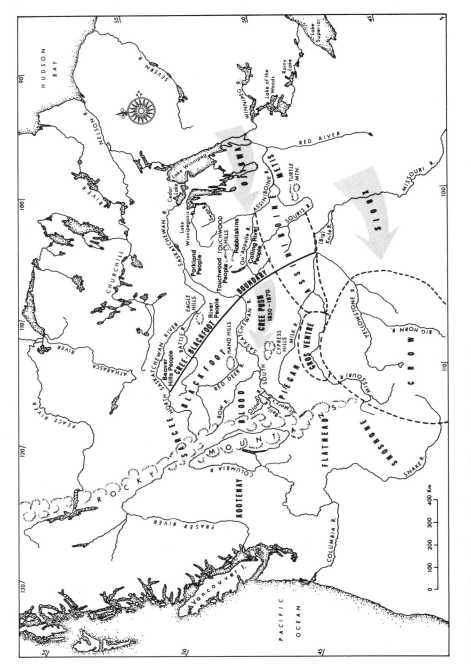

Map 1. Plains Indian tribal boundaries, ca. 1850 (map by Caroline Trottier)

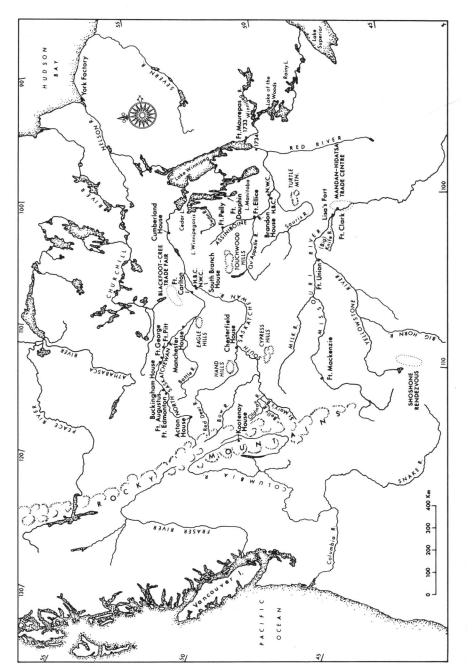

Map 2. Indian trade and fur-trade centres (map by Caroline Trottier)

Preface

This work, preliminary to a full tribal history, presents a reconstruction of a basic Plains Cree military and trade chronology of the period between 1790 and 1870. It concentrates on sifting historical evidence to isolate events in that sequence, using interpretation in a rather limited way, largely, although not exclusively, employing it to place these events in their proper time relationships and to provide some explanations of trade and military patterns as they emerge. In a sense these patterns, the trade and military networks involving the Cree and other plains people, the Blackfoot, Gros Ventre, Assiniboine, Mandan, Hidatsa, Crow and others, are equally important subjects of this study. They reveal an Indian side of the fur-trade era, a plains world of Indian creation that absorbs Europeans and their technology as another part of an aboriginal environment.

A tribe, rather than the networks of military, diplomatic and trade connections, is the most appropriate focus for study, however. The tribe defined the widest limit of plains social and political organization. Plains Indian life was tribal; it was as members of a tribe that they met, traded with, fought with and made peace with others, whether the others were Indians or Europeans. It is true that the concept *tribe* is rather amorphous. Plains tribes were not monolithic, wholly integrated structures. Cross-tribal, inter-familial connections at times blurred tribal demarcation lines, and the distance between bands of a plains tribe sometimes led to diverse participation in different, if rarely conflicting, trade and military systems. These factors stressed the oft-times decentralized, functional nature of the tribe and, with other considerations, have led scholars into an active debate over the utility of the concept and whether a regional or ethnic approach might be more useful. Despite these concerns, there is an overriding consideration that justifies, and indeed demands, a tribal approach. It is as tribes, or as tribal nations in the current parlance, that contemporary native people see themselves and wish to understand their past. The Plains Cree people are no exception. They have a right to their history, as all people have.

The choice of the Plains Cree, rather than some other plains tribe, is based on personal interest only. The Assiniboine, Plains Ojibwa and the members of the Blackfoot Confederacy are all equally deserving of attention.

The time span of the study, that is between 1790 and 1870, is not a personal whim. In this period the Cree people became a nation of the plains amid other tribal nations identifying their interests and employing the tools of trade, diplomacy and war to serve them. Their history is in fact distinguished by this national development, by epochs of defined economic interests and by utilitarian trade and military systems. Far from being the romantic and wild raiders of the plains, the Cree and other natives of the plains were engaged in a set of well-structured, inter-tribal relationships which were designed to ensure their security, to assist them in meeting the challenges of plains existence and to facilitate the acquisition of the good things of their world. Acquisition was a mainspring of their existence, and thus plains tribes were aggressive and fiercely competitive in inter-communal and inter-personal relations. Their history has a hard shell of war and sharp bargaining. But it also has a softer interior. To have was to share. Sharing, an economic necessity in the Woodland Cree environment, was a well-rewarded virtue in the Plains Cree world of buffalo plenty. Within the circle of tents that marked a band at rest was a system of redistribution which blunted the material consequences of an individual's failure in trade or the hunt, ensured the care and training of the young, and eased the burden of sorrow, the inescapable consequence of war and old age.

In this brief period (less than a century), the Plains Cree culture appeared, flourished and saw its independence wither and die along with the old fur-trade West. However, the full span of relevant history begins not only when the Cree's woodland ancestors adopted a plains way of life in the 1790s, but with the advent of the European fur trade in the seventeenth century. It was the fur trade, and perhaps the concomitant spread of European disease, which was the key dynamic of the Woodland Cree's migration into the western parkland and plains regions. It was the fur trade, in the main, that established the context for their initial relationships with other aboriginal people who became friends or enemies, partners or rivals, both in the woodland and in the subsequent days of plains existence. As such, the woodland, fur-trade-related experience of the Cree, an experience which became intense with the opening of the Hudson's Bay Company (HBC) posts on the bayside after 1670, forms an indispensible prologue to Plains Cree history.

This longer period, from 1670 to 1870, has a particular chronological conformation. It begins with contact; it ends with the disappearance of the buffalo from Cree lands. Within this period there are three distinct eras, each characterized by a paramount motive for war – the wars of migration and territory which set the western economic and military stage upon which the emerging Plains Cree nation would play out its existence, the horse wars covering the "golden years" of plains Indian life, and the buffalo wars which mark the sorrowful trail to the reserves. Intimately related to each era is a particular trade pattern supported by a parallel military system that linked the Cree with other plains tribes and with non-natives. These three eras and their distinctive trade and military patterns provide the structure for this work.

In the first era, from 1670 to the early nineteenth century, the Cree were most closely connected with the spread of the European fur trade. With the Assiniboine they became middlemen, expanding from the Bay along the prairie and parkland river systems, purveying European goods to inland tribes, and trapping for prime furs. The benefit they derived from this activity is seen not only in their monopolistic relationship with the isolated HBC traders at the bayside, but also in the manner in which Cree traders were able to operate successfully within the context of existing political and economic realities in the interior. The Blackfoot-Cree alliance, which began to take shape in the early 1730s and was still a feature of plains politics eighty years later, saw the Cree take advantage of Blackfoot preoccupation with a war against the Snake. The Cree, wisely, became suppliers of military ware – European weapons – which effectively tipped the balance of power in favour of the Blackfoot. Similarly, in the southeastern Canadian plains region, Cree and Assiniboine traders formed a coordinated trade and military relationship with the Mandan and Hidatsa, whose villages became the focus of an extensive native trade system.

Not only did the Cree penetrate to the plains region in this era and participate in the creation and operation of trade and military patterns, but they also underwent, from the 1790s on, a profound social transformation that saw the evolution of a Plains Cree culture. The canoe-reliant Cree traders became horse-owning, parkland-prairie dwellers. There again, the Cree responded positively to existing circumstances. In this case the inland extension of European fur posts, the consequent rise in the opportunity for provision trading and the availability of horses moved many Cree to abandon the prime role of fur trapping and trading and to take up buffalo hunting and what Company traders described as the idleness of that way of life.

This era came to an end with a dramatic realignment in military and trade patterns as a consequence of the changes in fur-trade organization and this social transformation. Old systems with the Blackfoot and with the Mandan-Hidatsa disintegrated violently, and the Cree were forced to find new ones to replace them.

The new patterns which were formed in the second era, lasting through to the middle of the century, focussed on what was of greatest importance to the emerging Plains Cree nation and to plains people in general – horses. Indeed, both the Blackfoot-Cree alliance and the Cree-Assiniboine relationship with the Mandan-Hidatsa failed on the issue of horse trading. The efforts of the Plains Cree thereafter were devoted to securing a reliable supply by gaining entry to southern horse markets. Trade systems, involving the Crow and others, brought with them the need to participate in supportive military activity. Trade and war were bound together anew. Campaigns in this period were directed primarily against the Blackfoot and seemed to advance the consolidation of the Plains Cree, as bands from across the plains, from Edmonton and from the Red River area, took part. Forays by small groups of warriors to steal Blackfoot horses or "tribal" strikes to answer or counter Blackfoot assaults provided an annual summer rhythm to Plains Cree life.

By the middle of the century, this rhythm was disturbed as the attention of plains Indians was drawn to a grave fact: the vast buffalo herds, the basis of life, were diminishing. In the early 1830s American traders along the Missouri had raised the price paid for buffalo robes and began to trade repeating rifles. This had thrown plains Indians into a ferocious assault on the herds. By 1850, the start of this last and shortest era, the Plains Cree felt this crisis early and hard, since the buffalo disappeared first from their region, remaining in numbers only in southwestern Alberta – Blackfoot territory.

The Plains Cree responded in two ways. The first was most significant in view of the eventual meeting of Plains Cree chiefs and Canadian government negotiators in the mid-1870s: they established a public position on their territory, their nation's land, declaring it their resource area, and preventing, to the extent that they could, incursions by others, Métis and whites included. The nation was more than an ethnic identity. It was also a specific place.

The second response was a sign of the increasing desperation of the situation: they began an armed migration. They attempted to expand their territory westward to reach the buffalo herds. In various tribal campaigns they strove to smash through to the buffalo, but these campaigns came to nought, with a crushing defeat in 1870. Thereafter the Plains Cree obtained buffalo through the charity of the victorious Blackfoot.

The threefold division of the chronology determines more than the structure of this volume. It also determines the character. The concentration on military and trade patterns dictates that other factors remain relatively unexplored or are utilized in a purposeful fashion. Demographic questions, issues such as the Cree system of social welfare, prestige and investment, and deterministic factors such as the impact of the horse and gun are discussed only insofar as they contribute to an understanding of the motives of war and trade and the development of those patterns. A broader social history tracing the evolution of cultural systems from the 1790s to 1870 is not attempted.

One area of especial concern that has had to be left unattended is that of women. This results primarily from the fact that the work focusses on trade and war – predominantly male activities. Native women, it is known, had an important internal economic role within the subsistence pattern as small-game hunters and gatherers, and a critical role related to trade as the "work force" that produced finished furs for exchange. Unfortunately, the "male"-oriented sources, both oral and documentary, provide little information that allows a reconstruction of Plains Cree women's experience and its integration into the trade and military patterns, and thus these women are yet hidden from history.

What is presented is a macro-historical approach to the Plains Cree in pre-reserve days in terms of their external relations. This perspective is given with as much precision as possible. There are limitations, however. For example, it has been impossible to determine the exact character of inter-tribal relations in every instance, particularly in the eighteenth century. The term *alliance* has been used to designate not only formal agreements and coordinated action by two or more parties against another, but also what might be termed *coincidental* activity by two parties, who may not have been formally allied, who took parallel action against a third. Coincidental activity might be a more accurate characterization, for example, of the Cree-Assiniboine relationship with the Mandan-Hidatsa in the eighteenth and early nineteenth centuries. The lack of primary sources is largely responsible for this impression. Unfortunately, fur-trade journalists did not attend many band council or inter-tribal meetings. Much took place on the far side of their fur-post horizon. It is possible, too, that a detailed historical analysis which concentrated on a shorter time period and a more limited geographic area and which examined, where evidence permitted, such factors as families and individuals and their roles in external affairs would establish a fuller perspective on some of these relationships.

None of the foregoing reservations, however, detract from the conviction underlying this work that a macro-historical approach concentrating on the unfolding chronology of military and trade patterns provides the most useful context for studies of more specific phenomena, including those of a social and cultural focus.

One further consideration has influenced the character of this work. I want to address students of Canadian native history, professional and lay, and in particular to reach Canadian historians responsible for the inclusion of Indian history in the general discussion, writing and, most important, the teaching of Canadian history. This consideration has dictated that the text itself be straightforward. The evolution of native history and of ethnohistory in recent times has tended to isolate native historians and their work from other historians, and has created a disciplinary language which can be appreciated only by the specialist. My desire to reach a wider audience, based on a belief that Canadian history will be incomplete until it pays due attention to the experience of native people, has dictated that the more esoteric debates of native history and ethnohistory be avoided as much as possible in the text. For those of an adventuresome inclination, gateways into some of these discussions are indicated in the footnotes.

This work is not, of course, alone in devoting attention to the Plains Cree. Others have gone before and, although the structure and character of this work is different, it is still indebted to them. Principal among these is David Mandelbaum's *The Plains Cree*. It still stands as the major anthropological source. Although not an attempt at a tribal history, A.J. Ray's regional study, *Indians in the Fur Trade,* is an invaluable guide for anyone undertaking work on Indians in western Canada. It demonstrates the benefits to be derived from the investigation of inter-tribal economic relations in the context of the fur trade, and is the pioneer work in that area. J.F. Dion's *My Tribe the Crees* and E. Ahenakew's *Voices of the Plains Cree* are to be treasured because, among other reasons, they indicate that the Plains Cree are as passionate as any other nation is about their past.

Finally, there is another debt, a personal one, which I owe to many people who have made this work possible. In particular I wish to thank Professor S.R. Mealing, who initiated the project, Professor G. Friesen, whose patience allowed the work to move forward, and Molly Blyth, who cleared the way for its completion. Above all I must thank Catherine Milloy, who in health and sickness supported my devotion to the Plains Cree.

The Plains Cree

Overleaf: Piapot, a Cree Indian chief, ca. 1800 (Glenbow Archives, Calgary, NA-532-1)

EVOLUTION AND REALIGNMENT

I

Overleaf: Cree Indian family with travois, near Calgary (Glenbow Archives, Calgary, NA-4035-87)

The Saskatchewan River Cree: Migration, War and Trade, 1690 to 1813

1

When the Plains Cree entered their reserves, the shadow they cast stretched back northeastward along a path nearly two centuries long. These Cree were men and women of enterprise, courage and determination. Their Woodland Cree ancestors had trekked westward from eastern Manitoba and northern Ontario in the seventeenth and eighteenth centuries, not just following opportunity, but also creating it. They built a new life and, indeed, a new western culture. In the late eighteenth century, principally on the banks of the Saskatchewan and Red rivers, a Plains Cree nation evolved.

This migration began with the fur trade. In the early seventeenth century, Woodland Cree were located in an area stretching from the Eastmain River to the Winnipeg River.[1] Through a southern connection with the Nipissing, they were in contact with the Montreal-based westward flow of European goods. At the distant end of the French fur-trade chain, the Cree received, in trade for prime quality fur, a restricted supply of dull knives, soiled cloth, torn nets and kettles worn thin by use. It is very unlikely that they acquired any firearms through this system.[2]

In the next quarter century, a dramatic change was wrought in Cree fur-trade fortunes, and with it came a dramatic change in their history. When the Hudson's Bay Company (HBC) opened its bayside posts between 1668 and 1688 on the doorstep of Cree territory, the Cree became the Company's chief consumers and merchandisers of European goods. It was an enviable position. They took control of the river systems which drained the West and hampered access to the posts to all western native residents except their allies, the Assiniboine.[3] Armed with muskets and iron-tipped weapons, they began a two-pronged western migration that brought them through the northern woodlands to the Rocky Mountains[4] and in a southwesterly direction to the great plains.

It is this latter southwestern penetration, with its own two tines, the Red River[5] and the Saskatchewan River system, that demands close attention, because it presents the most pertinent preamble to Plains Cree history. By this corridor, Cree trappers and traders not only came to a rich fur resource area and to their future homeland (what would be the territory of the Plains Cree nation), but also were brought into contact with the native group which played a most crucial role in Plains Cree history – the Blackfoot. The Blackfoot would be friend and enemy, trade partner and competitor. Blackfoot and Cree formed the first extensive native trade and military alliance on the western Canadian plains. Their relations, whether amicable or hostile, were the axis of western native politics from the seventeenth century, through the plains era and into this century. Their early relationship must be understood before the wars of migration and trade along the Saskatchewan River in the seventeenth and eighteenth centuries can be explained.

Despite the contention in many works that the Cree and Blackfoot were implacable enemies from their first meeting, the opposite is true.[6] Their initial relationship was an alliance founded on the coincidence of Cree economic and Blackfoot military interests. Prior to Cree penetration into the Saskatchewan River area, the Blackfoot had been driven out of southern Alberta by the Snake.[7] When Cree and retreating Blackfoot met, it was in friendship. The relevant tradition was related by one of the Blackfoot members, Weasel Tail, to anthropologist J.C. Ewers:

The Blackfoot began to acquire guns before they got horses. Before they had any guns, the bow and arrow was their principal weapon. They were then friendly with the Crees. One time a party of Blackfeet were in the woods north of the Saskatchewan. They heard a frightening noise and began to run away. Some Crees, who had made the noise by shooting a gun, motioned to the Blackfeet and told them to come to them. The Crees then showed the Blackfeet how to load a gun from the muzzle and to fire it by pulling the trigger.[8]

It appears that in this Blackfoot-Cree meeting the Cree did not shoot at the Blackfoot; instead, they taught the Blackfoot how to use guns. There is no indication, either in documentary evidence or oral tradition, that that friendly relationship changed in any significant fashion until the end of the eighteenth century.

It is impossible of course to discern when the first Cree-Blackfoot meeting took place. The earliest evidence, Henry Kelsey's journal, is sketchy and imprecise. It is certain, at least, that by 1690 both Cree and Assiniboine people, associated principally with York Factory, had expanded inland and were then familiar with, and were involved in, what was to become a permanent pattern, the exploitation of the plains area. Additionally, they were involved in a local military situation with a somewhat mysterious grouping: the Eagle Birch Indians, the Mountain Poets and the Naywattame Poets.[9] For reasons not now known, the Cree and some of their

Assiniboine allies were enemies of the Nayawattame Poets,[10] attacking them frequently.

After Henry Kelsey returned to York in 1692, Cree continued their migration south and southwestward. The state of warfare between the Cree-Assiniboine and the Gros Ventre (Naywattame Poets) continued. Cree relations with the Blackfoot remained friendly.

No further light is thrown on the progress of the Saskatchewan Cree until the early eighteenth century. In 1723 a sixteen-year-old Cree boy named Saukamappee was living with his family and their band somewhere on the Saskatchewan River east of the Blackfoot. Years later he related those times to fur trader David Thompson. Evidently, the Snake-Blackfoot war was still in progress. The Blackfoot, with the Piegan suffering the brunt of the Snake advance, had retreated northeast and were then to the east of the Eagle Hills.[11] In the winter of 1722, the Piegan sent out a call for help to all the tribes of the Blackfoot nation. Two messengers from the Piegan came to the camp of Saukamappee's father. Twenty Cree volunteered to aid the Blackfoot.[12]

We came to the Peeaganes and their allies. They were camped in the Plains on the left bank of the River (the north side) and were a great many. We feasted, a great war tent was made, and a few days passed in speeches. . . . A war chief was elected by the chiefs, and we got ready to march. Our spies had been out and had seen a large camp of the Snake Indians on the Plains of the Eagle Hill, and we had to cross the River in canoes, and on rafts, which are securely secured for our retreat. When we had crossed and numbered our men, we were about 350 warriors. They had their scouts out, and came to meet us. Both parties made a great show of their numbers, and I thought that they were more numerous than ourselves.[13]

The ensuing battle resulted in a draw, the weary contestants leaving the field without a decision.

The Snake had fought with arrows "headed with a sharp, smooth, black stone [Obsidian] which broke when it struck anything." There were no firearms involved in the fight. The Cree guns "were left at home for those who stayed behind to hunt."[14] Nor were there horses in either the Blackfoot or Snake contingents.

Saukamappee, his father and fellow volunteers returned home. The boy grew up, became a skilled hunter and married.

We had passed a winter together, when Messengers came from our allies to claim assistance. . . . By this time the affairs of both parties had much changed; we had more guns and iron headed arrows than before; but our enemies the Snake Indians and their allies [Flathead and Kootenay] had Misstutim (Big Dogs, that is Horses) on which they rode, swift as the Deer, on which they dashed at the Peeagans, and with their stone Pakamoggan [tomahawks] knocked them on the head, and thus they lost several of their best men. This news we did not well comprehend and it alarmed us, for we had no idea of Horses and could not make out what they were. Only three of us went and I should not have gone, had not my wifes relations frequently intimated, that her father's medicine bag would be honored by the scalp of a Snake Indian.[15]

The Cree again set out to join the Piegan. The account does not give the location of the Blackfoot camp nor of the ensuing battle. It is important to note that between the first battle in 1723 and this one in 1732 the Snake had acquired horses. They probably also adopted the military tactics of the large cavalry unit which became the mark of many plains battles. This strategy combined the element of surprise with the rapid, headlong rush at the enemy. It was sudden, swift, and under certain conditions deadly.

After their arrival at the Blackfoot camp, the war chief surveyed his warriors and "found between us and the Stone Indians we had ten guns and each of us about thirty balls, and powder for the war, and we were considered the strength of the battle."[16]

The combined force of Blackfoot, Cree and Assiniboine began their march and found that "the enemy was near in a large war party, but had no Horses with them, for at that time they had very few of them."[17]

These enemies quickly joined the battle. As in 1723, parallel lines were formed and the warriors hid behind large, thick shields. But this time the outcome was much different: "Our shots caused consternation and dismay along their whole line. The battle had begun about Noon, and the sun was not yet half down, when we perceived some of them had crawled away from their shields, and were taking to flight." The Snake had been routed. Great celebrations followed, honours were heaped upon the Cree and Assiniboine marksmen whose "guns had gained the victory." Saukamappee, who returned to live with the Blackfoot shortly after this battle, told Thompson that "the terror of that battle and our guns has prevented any more general battles, and our wars have since been carried by ambuscade and surprize of small camps, in which we have greatly the advantage, from the Guns, arrow shods of iron, long knives, flat bayonets and axes from the Traders."[18]

From 1732 to 1751 there is a break in the chain of evidence. It cannot be known for certain whether joint campaigns continued against the Snake in the Saskatchewan River area. The journal of La Vérendrye's sons who travelled southwest of the Missouri River in 1742 with Indians they called the Gens des Chevaux does, however, throw some light on Snake activity along the Missouri.

After marching a number of days with the Gens des Chevaux, the La Vérendrye group came to the Indians' main camp and found that the people "were in a state of great desolation. There was nothing but weeping and howling, all their villages having been destroyed by the Gens du Serpent [Snake Indians] and only a few of their tribe having escaped."[19]

These mounted Snake carried on their warfare from spring to fall. In 1741 it was claimed they had destroyed seventeen villages, killing old men and women, making slaves of the young women and trading them to the tribes of the seacoast for horses and Spanish goods.[20]

The La Vérendrye brothers then travelled on and joined a camp of Bow Indians who were on friendly terms with the Gens des Cheveaux.[21] They said: "Messages urging them [other bands] to meet us have been sent out in all directions. Every day you hear the war song chanted; this is not without purpose: we are going to march to the great mountains which are near the sea, to seek the Snakes there."[22] On New Year's Day 1743, the combined force of Bow and Gens des Cheveaux Indians came "in sight of the mountains. The number of warriors exceeded two thousand."[23]

The previously successful Snake raids had actually made that group vulnerable because various Missouri River people were compelled to join the list of tribes actively engaged against them. Not only had these actions increased the size of the forces attacking them, but also, possibly without knowing it, they had cut themselves off from the Mandan trading villages through which they could have received a supply of firearms in exchange for their horses. Had they been able to find their way into that trading system, they could have strengthened their position against the Cree and Blackfoot.

The Snake's contact with the Spanish was of little help to them in their dilemma: "The Spanish refuse to let them have firearms under pretense that these weapons will only induce them to kill each other." The Snake became isolated, aided only by their equally weak allies, the Kootenay and the Flathead. When explorers Lewis and Clark visited the Snake in 1805, Cameahwait, a chief, expressed the frustration and rage of his nation: "But this should not be, if we had guns, instead of hiding ourselves in the mountains and living like bears on roots and berries, we would then go down and live in the buffalo country in spite of our enemies, whom we never fear when we meet on equal terms."[24] Thus the Snake remained weak, ineffectual opponents, increasingly unable in the second half of the eighteenth century to hold back the southwestern thrust of the Blackfoot.

North of the Missouri in 1750, Legardeur de Saint Pierre noted that the Cree and Assiniboine were carrying on a successful series of campaigns against the "Hyactjlini, the Brochets and the Gros Ventres." Like Henry Kelsey, he tried to make peace among these nations. During the winter of 1750–51, he gathered these tribes together and they swore to live together as brothers. His success was shortlived, for in November 1751 he learned that some Assiniboine, who had been camping with the Hyactjlini, "seeing that they were much more numerous than the others, slaughtered them, and no mention made of a single person saved except a few women and children they carried off as prisoners."[25]

It is impossible to determine who the Hyactjlini and Brochet (Jackfish?) Indians were or even to be sure that these Gros Ventre were Fall or Rapid Indians. From evidence of a later date it seems doubtful that these Indians were of the Blackfoot nation. It is, of course, possible that these three Indian groups were all bands of the Gros Ventre nation.

Anthony Henday visited the far-western plains just three years after Legardeur de Saint Pierre did. In 1754 he found no evidence of Cree-Assiniboine hostilities against the Gros Ventre. His journal does give some hints on the condition of the Blackfoot-Cree alliance and the progress of their southwestern advance against the Snake and their allies. Travelling up the Saskatchewan by canoe and then across the plains, using a horse he had purchased from the Assiniboine, he reached a large encampment of Assiniboine near the site of Battleford, Saskatchewan, on 5 September 1754. He continued across the plains until he came to the junction of the Red Deer River and the South Branch of the Saskatchewan where he met the Archithinue (Blackfoot) Indians.[26]

Henday's mission – to convince these Indians to come down to York Factory – failed. They told him they didn't own or know how to use canoes. The trading which was carried on while Henday was in their village certainly indicates that they were receiving their supplies through the Cree and Assiniboine.[27]

It is also evident from Henday's journal that the Blackfoot had, by 1754, pushed the Snake, Kootenay and Flathead to a point southwest of the junction of the Red Deer River and South Branch of the Saskatchewan. Although no mention is made of battles, or even of the Snake, the cordial trading relations between the Cree-Assiniboine and Blackfoot were a probable indication that their military alliance was still operative.

Between Henday's visit in 1754 and the journey of Matthew Cocking in 1772, there is no direct documentary evidence relating to the Blackfoot-Cree warfare against the Snake. There is, though, an Indian tradition that discloses some of the military events during this period. Faro, a Flathead, related his recollection of the fate of his tribe in his boyhood to Warren Ferris, an American trader:

A great many snows past when I was a child our people were in a continual fear of the Black-feet, who were already in possession of firearms of which we knew nothing, save by their murderous effects. During our excursions for buffalo, we were frequently attacked by them, and many of our bravest warriors fell victims to the thunder and lightning they wielded which we conjectured had been given to them by the Great Spirit to punish us for our sins.[28]

Battle followed battle, with the Flathead suffering serious losses in each engagement:

They never came in reach of our arrows, but remained at such a distance that they could deal death to us without endangering themselves. . . . Goaded by thirst for revenge, we often rushed forth upon our enemies, but they receded like the rainbow in proportion as we advanced, and ever remained at the same distance, whence they destroyed us by their deadly bolts, while we were utterly powerless to oppose them.[29]

The Flathead soon realized that there was little they could do against the Blackfoot. They assembled in council, and Big Foot, the head chief of the nation, addressed them:

He set forth the necessity of leaving our country. "My heart tells me," said he, "that the Great Spirit has forsaken us; he has furnished our enemies with his thunder to destroy us, yet something whispers to me, that we may fly to the mountains and avoid a fate, which if we remain here is inevitable."[30]

The tribe listened to the voice whispering to Big Foot and began their retreat, leaving behind the plains and withdrawing into the protection of the mountains.

The extent of Cree involvement in these battles with the Flathead is unknown: Relations with the Blackfoot remained friendly through this period, so it is quite possible that some Cree were included.

On 24 August 1772, Matthew Cocking, travelling to the West with the same purpose in mind as had Anthony Henday, reached the South Branch of the Saskatchewan just south of its junction with the North Branch. His hunters, Assiniboine or Cree, "saw several Horses up the branch on the other side. They are all in general afraid, supposing the horses to belong to the Snake Indians with whom they are always at variance."[31] This reaction to the sighting of a strange horse was repeated a number of times during Cocking's trip. It is obvious that the Cree and Assiniboine had maintained their opposition to the Snake.

By 4 November 1772, Cocking had still not contacted the Blackfoot nation and he had lost hope of finding them. This was "a great disappointment to my companions who used to trade"[32] with them. He noted further in his description of the Blackfoot that they met the Cree-Assiniboine each March to carry on trade.[33] The Cree-Blackfoot relations obviously continued to be cordial; they had annual meetings, and the Blackfoot explored the real possibility that the Cree and/or Assiniboine accompany them on their war trips. It is likely that young Cree men did not devote themselves exclusively to trade but were drawn to war, motivated by concerns for status, by such inducements as their wives' "relations frequently [intimating] that her father's medicine bag would be honored by the scalp of a Snake Indian."[34]

Cocking had no more success in convincing the Blackfoot to come in to trade than had Henday. They gave him almost the same reason: the long and arduous journey and their lack of canoes. As they were parting he was told that "their Countrymen are going to war with the Snake Indians."[35]

The exact location of the Snake during this period is difficult to determine. Saukamappee does, however, provide information on this point and introduces the next major event in this military calendar. According to his account (around the year 1780), the Blackfoot were advancing southward in the vicinity of the Red Deer River. They attacked a Snake camp but, to their amazement, met little resistance; the inhabitants of the camp were all dying. Two days later smallpox broke out in Blackfoot lodges.[36]

War was no longer thought of, and we had enough to do to hunt and make provisions for our families, for in our sickness we had consumed all our dried provisions. . . . Our hearts were low and dejected, and we shall never be again the same people. To hunt for our families was our sole occupation and kill Beavers, Wolves and Foxes to trade our necessaries; and we thought of War no more, and perhaps would have made peace with them [the Snake] for they had suffered dreadfully as well as us and had left all this fine country of the Bow River to us.[37]

This epidemic swept the plains from west to east in the years between 1780 and 1782. The Blackfoot advance had taken them back to their original homeland – the Bow River country. The shock of the epidemic and the massive loss of life caused a lull in the war; the lull lasted until 1785, when Thompson recorded, "Five of our tents [were] pitched away to the valleys of the Rocky Mountains, up a branch of this River [the Bow] to hunt the Big Horn Deer," [38] the Blackfoot were ambushed and killed by a party of Snake Indians.[39] Immediately the Blackfoot began to prepare for war.

"Early in September 1787, a party of about two hundred and fifty warriors under the command of Kootana Appe went off to war on the Snake Indians; they proceeded southward near the east foot of the mountains and found no natives."[40]

It is possible, of course, that this expedition had just missed the Snake who were still wandering on the plains. But it seems definite that between 1787 and 1805 the Snake withdrawal was completed. In the latter year, Lewis and Clark noted in their journal that "within their [the Snake's] own recollection they formerly lived in the plains, but they have withdrawn into the mountains."[41]

The Snake allies, the Kootenay, seem to have retreated into the mountains in the same period. Duncan McGillivray, a North West Company trader at Fort George

(North Branch of the Saskatchewan), disclosed in 1795 that "the Coutonies have already made several attempts to visit us, but they have been always obstructed by their enemies and forced to relinquish their design with loss; . . . this year however it is reported that they intend obtaining a safe passage hither by bribing their enemies with Bands of Horses. Whether this method will succeed we cannot judge, but it is shrewdly suspected that a party will be formed to intercept as usual their progress to this quarter."[42] By 1807 the Kootenay definitely had withdrawn from the Canadian plains and that year David Thompson crossed the mountains to find them.

In their westward drive, the Blackfoot and their Cree and Assiniboine allies had taken more than eighty years to reach the Rockies. At the end of the period the southwestern plains had been cleared of the Snake, Kootenay and Flathead. During the same era, New France, and hence the French fur trade, had fallen. The North West Company and HBC had entered the West and leap-frogged each other in the construction of posts along the length of the Saskatchewan.

As the history of the westward drive is largely a story of the superiority of arms of one group of antagonists over the other, the story is not fully told until the drive was stopped and a new military pattern begun. By 1813 this new pattern was established and the balance of power levelled.

The movement of the Canadian and British traders along the Saskatchewan was matched, although on a smaller scale in the early nineteenth century, by the arrival of American fur traders at the western end of the Missouri. The Blackfoot quickly realized the danger of Americans crossing the mountains and entering into trade with the Snake and Flathead. They effectively blockaded the sources of the Missouri and adopted a policy of indiscriminately killing Americans on sight.[43] They employed a similar policy of blockade on the Saskatchewan[44] but they implemented it with more caution, never going further than threats. To kill a white person in the Saskatchewan area would have threatened their own supply of firearms.

In 1807 Thompson evaded the Saskatchewan blockade, crossed the mountains and began the first direct trade with the Kootenay at Kootenay House. The Kootenay were quick to take advantage of Thompson's presence and the subsequent arrival of other traders. Before the traders had established contact, the Kootenay had nurtured a burning hatred against the fur traders for supplying their enemies with firearms that had been used to drive them from their ancestors' lands. Yet, when the traders came, "they appeared to be perfectly aware that the beaver was the only object that induced us [Ross Cox of the North West Company] to visit their country; and they accordingly exerted themselves to procure it, not, as some of them candidly declared for our interest, but for the purpose of obtaining firearms, spears to enable them to meet their old enemies the Blackfeet on more equal terms."[45]

Thompson suggested that there was an additional factor connected with their acquisition of firearms, which certainly supplemented the new strength of the Kootenay:

All those who could procure Guns soon became good shots; . . . the Peegan Indians. . . are not good shots they are accustomed to fire at the Bison on horseback, within a few feet of the animal, it gives them no practice at long shots at small marks. On the contrary, the Indians on the west side of the Mountains are accustomed to fire at the Small Antelope at a distance of one hundred and twenty yards, which is a great advantage in battle, where everyone marks out his man.[46]

When the Piegan realized that Thompson had slipped through their blockade, they crossed the mountains, found the post, lay siege to it for three weeks, and then departed. Their civil chief was incensed by these events. He "harangued them, and gave his advice to form a strong war party under Kootonai Appie the War Chief and directly to crush the white Men and the Natives on the west side of the Mountains before they became well armed. They have always been our slaves and now they will pretend to equal us; no, we must not suffer this, we must at once crush them. We know them to be desperate Men, and we must destroy them before they become to [sic] powerful for us."[47] This Piegan chief fully understood the dangers. They had whipped the Kootenay into submission and driven them across the mountains. Now the Kootenay were turning around to face them, desperate for revenge and armed with the same weapon the Blackfoot had used to defeat them. He knew it was only a matter of time before the Kootenay struck back. The Blackfoot had to crush them before they were ready.

/ Between 1807 and 1812, the Kootenay received a regular supply of arms, although the Piegan attempted to enforce their blockade through to 1811.[48] Blackfoot annoyance with the white traders for supplying arms to their enemies grew with their inability to stop the westward flow of guns. It reached a critical point in 1812./

/ James Bird (an HBC trader) noted in the Edmonton post journal of that year that "the Muddy River Indians [Piegans] sent, lately, Young Men to his House [Acton House, an HBC Post close to the Rockies] . . . to inform them that the Blood Indians were determined in attacking both Houses [Acton and the North West Company post in the area] on Account of a Defeat they had lately received from an Enemy, who was assisted by White Men."[49] This turned out to be a desperate threat. The Blood Indians restricted their actions to stealing the traders' horses. Regardless, the arming of the Kootenay continued.

Finally, after years of defeats, the Kootenay began to enjoy the fruits of victory. Probably the choicest of these was their ability to recross the mountains to hunt the buffalo in the land that had once been theirs.[50] In 1812 the Piegan sued for peace but negotiations broke down and the warfare continued.[51]

On 24 December 1813, Ross Cox reported a significant event in the history of the Flathead people. A large band of Flathead warriors "had recently returned from the buffalo country, and had revenged their defeat of the preceding year by a signal victory over their enemies the Blackfeet, several of whose warriors, with their women, they had taken prisoners."[52] The victory surely gave them hope that they could recross the mountains each summer and hunt the buffalo in relative safety, in order to procure a supply of dried meat for the winter.

Like their Kootenay neighbours, the Flathead had been overjoyed at the opportunity of purchasing arms from the traders who arrived on their side of the mountains. Cox described the turn in Flathead fortunes which followed: "From this moment affairs took a decided change in their favour, and in their subsequent contests the numbers of killed, wounded, and prisoners were more equal."/The Blackfoot, on the other hand, were furious and they declared "to our people [North West Company employees] at Forts des Praires [Saskatchewan River posts] that all white men who might happen to fall into their hands, to the westward of the mountains, would be treated by them as enemies, in consequence of their furnishing the Flatheads with weapons, which were used with such deadly effect against their nation."[53]/

Perhaps the final point in the re-emergence of Flathead and Kootenay power was the rebirth in 1813 of their former alliance. They agreed "that neither party shall make peace with the Blackfeet until the latter shall permit them to hunt without molestation on the buffalo plains."[54] They also began to make joint trips to the buffalo grounds in an attempt to ensure the security of their hunting parties.[55]

The Snake, too, began to receive arms. They did not at this point join the Flathead-Kootenay alliance. Rather, they added the Nez Perce to their long list of adversaries and began to look for a peace settlement with the Blackfoot.[56]

The arming of the Kootenay, Flathead and Snake, and the formation of the Flathead-Kootenay alliance, did not prevent the Blackfoot from continuing to conduct their raids across the mountains for scalps and horses. But it did ensure that the Blackfoot could no longer raid without fear of serious losses, and that the Snake, Flathead and Kootenay could hunt on the plains with some hope of defending their hunting parties. The new strength of these tribes, and the formation and continued existence of their alliance, play an important part in Blackfoot-Cree relations and general plains-Indian history throughout the rest of the fur-trade period.

* * *

It is important now to look at Blackfoot-Cree relations from a non-military perspective. To fully understand the Cree support of the Blackfoot territorial drive in the eighteenth century, it is essential to appreciate the economic opportunity that the Cree identified, and took advantage of, in the Blackfoot-Snake hostilities.

While it is difficult to assess the frequency of front-line participation of the Cree in the Blackfoot drive to the mountains, there is little doubt that the major part played by the Cree in those military events was in supplying the Blackfoot with firearms. If there was one thing that Saukamappee and Cameahwait, the Snake chief, agreed on, it was that the introduction of the gun and iron-headed shock weapons tipped the military scale in favour of the Canadian plains tribes who had established contact with the British traders. Considering the fact that the Cree and their Assiniboine allies were supplying European weapons to the Missouri River Indians through the Mandan-Hidatsa villages, and to the Blackfoot nation, their economic significance in the northern plains region is understandable and deserves further attention.

To suggest that the Cree, in their favoured trade position, simply blocked other tribes from gaining access to the fur-trade posts is to suggest that the Cree did not know how to maximize the benefits of their geographic position. In the plains area, throughout the eighteenth century, the Cree manifested the behaviour of traders in every sense: they practised sharp bargaining with their European sources and set a very high tariff on the goods they brought to their Indian trading partners.

Even though the British and the French were their indispensable suppliers, the Cree were not tied to a particular British or French trade policy. The pleadings of La Vérendrye, Legardeur de Saint Pierre and Kelsey for a peace that would benefit the trade fell on uncooperative and independent ears. It was the Cree who decided who would and would not receive goods from the Europeans.[57] In this regard Cree trade and military policies went hand in hand. From the 1690s all through the eighteenth century, the Naywattame-Gros Ventre were excluded by the Cree, who hunted and attacked them seemingly at every opportunity. When the Blackfoot-Cree military alliance began to break down, the Cree were quick to turn to the aid of their former enemy, the Flathead.[58]

For some reason, the Cree chose to enter into a military and trade relationship with the Blackfoot. When and by whom the decision was taken, and exactly when the trading began, is not known. Saukamappee's account suggests that the military cooperation pre-dates the trade system, or, more precisely, that it pre-dates the inclusion of the gun as a commodity in that system. As late as the second battle in 1732 the Blackfoot, he claims, did not have firearms.[59] Even after that engagement the Blackfoot remember receiving guns as marriage gifts but not as articles of trade.[60] Weasel Tail states that "the Blackfoot began to acquire guns before they got horses."[61] This would date the beginning of the Cree-Blackfoot trade in guns to a point between 1732 and 1754 when Henday visited the Blackfoot and found that the Blackfoot and the Assiniboine had horses.[62] Initially the Blackfoot received their horses by stealing them from the Snake,[63] the Kootenay and the Flathead, who in turn acquired them from the South in the area of the Spanish settlements.[64] It was the desire for horses, as well as the historic territorial grievance, that inspired Blackfoot campaigns against their enemies.

Anthony Henday was the first white person to see the Blackfoot-Cree trading process. On 15 May 1755 he began to trade with the Blackfoot and "the Indians [Cree and Assiniboine] purchased great numbers of Wolves, Beaver and Foxes . . . which proves what the Woman formerly told me concerning the Natives getting part of their Furs from the Archithinue [Blackfoot] Indians."[65] This was the core of that trade system. Cree traders visited the Blackfoot in the spring and supplemented their own winter hunts taken along the Saskatchewan River with the furs that the Blackfoot had collected. They then turned east and began the long journey to York Fort.

Like other Cree arriving from the northern interior, they would have been determined to make the best trade possible; they demanded fair dealing. In a typical pre-trading speech, the captain of the Indians exhorted the traders: "tell your servants to fill the measure, and not to put their thumbs within the brim. . . . Let us trade good black tobacco, moist and hard twisted; let us see it before it is opened. . . . Let the young men have more than measure of tobacco, cheap kettles, thick, and high." If the goods were not of sufficient quality they complained. They returned guns that had exploded in their hands. They demanded "light guns, small in the hand, and well shaped, with locks that will not freeze in the winter."[66]

After completing their trade at the Bay, the Cree returned to the Saskatchewan to spend the winter hunting before again visiting the Blackfoot. This rhythm of trade by which the Cree lived was duplicated by the HBC when it had built its inland posts.

Matthew Cocking in 1772 designated March as the month of the Cree-Blackfoot trade mart and suggested that the area just southwest of the junction of the North and South branches of the Saskatchewan was to be the location.[67] He noted that the Cree and Assiniboine received "horses and Buffalo skin garments, for winter apparel also wolf skins and other furs"[68] from the Blackfoot. He did not, though, enumerate the goods the Blackfoot acquired in exchange. Andrew Graham, an HBC employee, provided valuable additional details of Cree trading activities. According to his account a Blackfoot made his way to York Factory in 1766: "I asked him if there were any beaver and wolves etc. in his country. He said there were plenty and that our traders [Cree] came amongst them and bought up their furs."[69] Graham learned that the list of trade goods included in addition to guns, hatchets, kettles and knives.[70] Powder and shot should be added to this list as well as "arrow shods of iron, long knives, [and] bayonets."[71]

Of much greater significance was Graham's discovery of the prices charged to the Blackfoot by those Cree traders. From his remarks on this, and the Company's standard at that time, one can compare prices (see Table 1). The Blackfoot hunter was allowed to substitute wolves in the same amount as beaver to purchase these articles from the Cree. The high price for guns is understandable. The Blackfoot were a captive market and they derived direct economic and military benefit from having guns. With them, their attacks on the Snake were successful, and the horses they took as booty could be traded to the Cree and Assiniboine. There is only one note in the early sources on the price of horses in the Cree-Blackfoot trading system. Henday, in 1754, purchased a horse from a member of an Assiniboine band to the southwest of Battleford, Saskatchewan, for a gun.[72] Using the Cree tariff of 1766, this would make a horse purchased in that area worth about fifty beaver. This, of course, can only be accepted as a rough estimate.

The state of warfare on the western plains at any given time dictated both the type and quantity of articles traded. Obviously, a heavy emphasis was ascribed to European tools of war: guns, knives and arrow heads. As these were the goods for which the demand was highest, and consequently so was the price, other, lower-priced articles played a minor part in the trade system. This may explain why, in 1772, the Blackfoot were still making and using their own pottery to "dress their victuals." Among the Assiniboines living in the same area as the Blackfoot, and who were probably being serviced by Cree traders, Alexander Henry (the Elder) found the same situation. They too were poor in kettles. "Our supper was made on the tongues of the wild ox, or buffalo, boiled in my kettle which was the only one in the camp,"[73] of two hundred tents.

The Cree were not destined to remain the sole provisioners of the Blackfoot. By 1776 the Canadian traders had reached the Forks of the Saskatchewan River.[74] Between 1774 and 1799 the HBC had posts stretching from the mouth of the Saskatchewan to the source of the North Branch in the Rocky Mountains. The Canadian traders had a post at almost every HBC location. However, the Cree-Blackfoot trade system did not cease immediately. The predominantly eastern location of early Saskatchewan posts, the irregular visits of Canadians, the uncertainty of their supplies, and even the short supplies of the HBC when it reached the Saskatchewan, probably allowed the Cree to act as a supplementary source. These shortages, plus Cree involvement in beaver trapping which other tribes passed up in favour of exclusive concentration on the buffalo hunt, provided the Cree with added buying power, allowing them to continue in their former role. For many years

TABLE 1
Goods and Prices of Articles Traded by the HBC and the Cree, and by the Cree and Blackfoot (1766)

Article	HBC Price for Cree	Cree Price for Blackfoot
1 gun	14 beaver	50 beaver
1 hatchet	1 beaver	6 beaver
1 large kettle	8 beaver	20 beaver
1 knife	1/3 beaver	4 beaver

Note: G. Williams, *Andrew Graham's Observations on Hudson Bay, 1767–1791* (London:
The Hudson Bay Record Society, 1969), 257. Additional information on tariffs can be
found in A.J. Ray, *Indians in the Fur Trade* (Toronto: University of Toronto Press, 1974),
69.

they continued to trade guns for horses with the Assiniboine[75] and probably with
the Blackfoot, too, while their relations remained friendly.

Over a long period, then, the Cree-Blackfoot trade system acted as the vital basis
of their military alliance. Even the yearly trapping-trading schedule which brought
fresh supplies to the Saskatchewan plains every spring coincided with the prosecution by the Blackfoot of campaigns during the summer months.

It has been remarked that the Cree middlemen prevented others from reaching
the British bayside posts. Although this may be true in the case of the Naywattame
and others, it is an irrelevant concept in the case of the Blackfoot. Anthony Henday once commented that the Cree, though they had "promised the Chief Factor at
York Fort to talk to them [the Blackfoot] strongly on that Subject [to convince the
Blackfoot to come to trade at the Bay], they never opened their mouths."[76] This
should not be interpreted, despite Henday's view, as the reluctance of the middleman to give up his position. It is indicative of the understanding between the Cree
and Blackfoot. The latter were neither able to go east nor did they wish to. After
all, they were not in desperate need of kettles. What they needed, and indeed
received, from their Cree allies were arms – the extra margin of force which enabled
them to drive back their Snake, Kootenay and Flathead enemies.

Throughout the period of their alliance with the Blackfoot, the Cree organized
and maintained their economic system. They hunted, prepared and bought skins
with which they acquired goods to trade with Indians who did not have direct contact with the European supplier. Their system was doubly advantageous to them,
for they could realize benefit at either end of the trade chain. The margin on
European goods sold to the Blackfoot could be utilized at the fur posts for purchasing luxury items: extra kettles, liquor, decorative items such as buttons and bells,
or more guns and iron weapons. Or, they could transport a supply of weapons to

the Blackfoot and purchase the one item they could not receive in the European fur trade – the horse.

The horse, however, had no economic benefit within the trade system (unless traded further east at higher prices) until the traders came to build their posts along the prairie's rim. Only then did the provision trade become a profitable venture for ex-middlemen Cree, and only then was the horse a common economic asset for trading, buffalo hunting and the transportation of dried meat.

Despite its utility, the Cree-Blackfoot trade and military system would not survive the first decade of the nineteenth century. The increasing presence of white traders along the Saskatchewan set the stage for fundamental economic, political and even social change in this area. The Cree response to this threat to their position as middleman combined horse ownership with the economic opportunities of buffalo hunting. In turn, this re-orientation launched the Cree on a transition – a social transformation which saw the appearance of a Plains Cree people. This new nation would have to adjust its relationship with the traders, the Blackfoot and other tribes. In this process old systems, such as the Cree-Blackfoot alliance, would disintegrate and new ones would be formulated.

The Plains Cree:
The 1790s

2

One of the most difficult problems facing a Plains Cree historian is to date and explain the emergence of a plains variety of Cree culture. Numerous Woodland Cree had come to the Saskatchewan plains area as part of the western expansion after 1690. These Saskatchewan River Cree people had exploited the plains as a resource area and entered trade and military alliances with the Blackfoot that spanned the eighteenth century. When, however, and for what reasons, did many of them adopt what was identified by fur traders in the early nineteenth century as a plains way of life? The problem is a complex one, for it demands not only the establishment of a time frame for this transition, but also the reconstruction, in part, of a process of social transformation.

An early attempt to provide an answer to the problem, a work by A.S. Morton, highlights some of the associated difficulties that must be confronted. Morton suggested that, "at an early date Crees wandered onto the prairies and adopted the very different manner of living which characterized the buffalo country."[1] Unfortunately, this explanation, with its implied environmental determinant and suggestion that the Cree adopted some classic or standard mode of plains existence, is, upon examination, far from clear or precise. The "buffalo country" (buffalo range) encompassed not only the prairie but the parklands as well. This range was, in turn, part of a larger and more complex ecology comprising, generally from north to south, woodland, parkland and grassland zones. It was shared, from time immemorial through to treaty time (the 1870s), by native groups of diverse type. The "transitional parkland belt"[2] contained the widest range of food resources and thus was attractive to and exploited by all, particularly in the winter months. In addition, the separate seasonal and cyclical variation in food supplies in the woodland, parkland and plains habitats were complementary. Woodland summer plenty, marked by an

'transitional parkland belt', rich, shared by various groups; seasonal complementary abundance of fish and wildfowl, was followed by mid-winter scarcities that brought the threat of starvation. Parkland winter resources, with the retreat of the buffalo seeking shelter from storms out on the plains, were plentiful just when woodland resources were scarce. The grassland cycle was much like that of the woodland, with summers of plenty followed by chilling and barren winters. These complementary, interlocking ecological zones drew plains and woodland bands across the wider area, exploiting as many as "two or three major environmental zones on a seasonal basis."[3]

This multi-zone pattern of resource exploitation held for the Plains Cree throughout the historic period. Spring saw them move out onto the prairie where they spent the summer hunting buffalo. When the nip of autumn was felt, they headed back to the protection of the parkland woods.[4]

Obviously, the buffalo country supported more than one "different manner of living." Woodland and plains people cohabited in a common place but were not, therefore, forced into a narrow common lifestyle. There were even differences in social structure and customs amongst plains people – the Blackfoot, Cree and Assiniboine; and there were marked differences between them and plains-agriculturalists – the Mandan and Métis, for example. Indeed, even within plains groups, there was not a single uniform lifestyle. There were those Plains Cree who, as late as the 1860s, showed a greater propensity for the woodlands than did others. They

... never completely abandoned their woodland ways and were content to live off fish and small game during the cold weather. Others in the camp were pure plainsmen who would disdain to eat moose or deer and considered buffalo to be the only proper food for an Indian. If the winter was mild, they ventured onto the edge of the plains to live off the herds and remained there as long as the weather would allow. Some stayed away all winter, but those in Big Bears band usually preferred the safety and comfort of the woodlands.[5]

To the many social-structural differences among member groups of the plains community must be added the differences of periods. Because these were human societies, ways of life changed from Morton's "early date" until the profoundly new epoch of reserve life in the 1870s. The introduction of the horse and gun, the arrival of European traders, the expansion of inter-tribal contact, the spread of disease, and the introduction of repeating rifles – all elements of the plains experience in the historic period – must be weighed as causal factors in plains cultural development. Their effects would not be the same, necessarily, for each plains society. There were, therefore, not only different plains ways of life at any one time, but there was also a series of different plains ways of life over the years. There were, then, epochs of Plains Cree culture.

Clearly, it is impossible to define a single "manner of living which characterized the buffalo country," to determine a standard model of plains existence. It is, therefore (to return to the specific problem of dating and explaining the origin of the Plains Cree nation), impossible to trace the evolution of Saskatchewan Cree woodland society to such a model of living; it is impossible to fully delineate such a process of social transformation.

The problem, however, can be approached from another direction and along a narrower front. It is possible to note some of the behavioural and cultural indicators of the Saskatchewan River Cree and to show that these changed, and when they changed, to what are commonly accepted as plains traits: for example, horse ownership, a particular relationship to the buffalo, and a new one with the European traders. This method will produce neither a model of the Saskatchewan River Cree nor of the infant Plains Cree society, but since the task is to isolate the date and explain the change from woodland to plains existence, it is not a drawback.

The term *Saskatchewan River Cree* is employed to designate those Woodland Cree who used the Saskatchewan River rather than the Nelson-Churchill-English river system as their route to the West after contact with the traders. They had a number of clear, distinguishing features. Perhaps the most prominent was their energy and deep involvement in the fur trade. They were the key element in the fur-gathering systems of the HBC and the French traders. They were not only trappers but also traders. Their relationship with the Blackfoot showed their considerable entrepreneurial talent. Like the European traders, they placed the highest value on the beaver. Finally, emphasis must be placed on their use of the canoe in the fulfillment of their fur-trading role. The canoe allowed quick, long-distance transportation and, hence, extensive penetration of the West. It would be misleading to suggest that these Saskatchewan River Cree had ever had a place of permanent occupation. Certainly, they had trapping areas in the Saskatchewan region. But their middleman role connected them to Hudson Bay and drew them back there each spring.

By 1690 these Cree were in contact with the plains and regularly were using them as a resource area. Henry Kelsey, in 1691, witnessed their buffalo hunt – one of the most colourful events in the lives of the plains Indians. In his journal, Kelsey describes Cree and Assiniboine hunters sighting a herd of buffalo: "When they see a great parcel of them they surround them with men wch done they gather themselves into a smaller Compass keeping ye Beast still in ye middle so shooting ym till they breakout at some place or other & so gett away from ym."[6] Further journal entries clearly establish these Cree as woodland Indians.

The pattern established by the Saskatchewan Cree of exploiting both woodland and plains and trading furs as well seems to have continued for a considerable period. The evidence is not conclusive, however. In 1723 when Saukamappee, his father and other Cree warriors went to the aid of the Blackfoot, his band was situated somewhere to the east or north of the Blackfoot area. They travelled to the Blackfoot camp by canoe, thus maintaining the ability to get back to York Fort. Furthermore, the Piegan messengers came to the Cree band in the winter of 1722.[7] The Cree pattern of living along the Saskatchewan in the winter and trapping that area before trading with the Blackfoot, and then returning to the Bay in the spring and summer was consistent with the yearly schedule of the Saskatchewan River Cree middlemen.

La Vérendrye was the first European to state that there were Cree on the plains. He noted in 1739 that the building of Fort Dauphin (Lake Winnipegosis near the mouth of the Red Deer River) had been requested by the Cree of the Prairies and the Canoe Assiniboine.[8] Unfortunately, there is no supportive evidence for this claim and he gives no description of these Cree. It is almost impossible to draw any conclusions from his statement.

However, the author of the most well-known Canadian-Indian history, E.P. Patterson, accepts La Vérendrye's statement at face value. He wrote: "By the 1730s some of the Cree were permanently out on the Prairies." Certainly, it is true that by the 1730s these Cree had established contact with the plains, but this had happened as early as the 1690s. If plains contact and other parallel factors such as buffalo hunting and trapping the area did not create plains residents, then some new factor must have appeared between 1690 and 1730 to keep some Cree "permanently out on the Prairies."[9]

Patterson can hardly argue that the Cree by the 1730s were abandoning canoes in favour of horses, for he holds, rather curiously, that the "Crees probably first acquired horses in the 1770s, the more westerly bands getting them before those in the east."[10] Yet, the appearance of the horse on the Canadian plains and Cree access to them, at an earlier date than the one Patterson suggests, may have been the new factor which initiated movement from forest to plain.

It was noted by Saukamappee that, although the Blackfoot had seen horses by 1732, they did not own any themselves.[11] When Henday visited the Blackfoot (1754–55) he found them well-mounted. But of greater significance, he noted that the Assiniboine in that area had horses and had maintained their ability to go to York Fort. On 17 May 1755 he recorded the following: "Ten tents of Eagle Indians joined the Architinue Indians. Five canoes of them are going to the Fort with me. They are a tribe of the Assinepoet Nation; and like them use Horses for carrying the baggage and not to ride on."[12]

A number of interesting patterns emerge from this. One is the initial use of the horse as a pack animal rather than as a mount. More critical is the fact that by 1754 the Blackfoot had acquired enough horses to be trading them. Some of the Assiniboine, if for no reason other than the necessity of tending the horses, would remain in the Saskatchewan River area, while others returned to York Factory for supplies.

Matthew Cocking's journal supports the existence of this Assiniboine pattern. On 19 September 1772, he "smoked with some Assinepoet strangers: I advised them to be diligent in trapping furs; and to go with me to the Company's Forts, most of them being strangers; but they seemed unwilling, saying, they were unacquainted with the method of building canoes and paddling: However they would send their furs by their friends who yearly visit the forts."[13] Cocking also stated that his Indian travelling companions (Assiniboine and Cree) "used to trade Horses"[14] with the Blackfoot. Alexander Henry (the Elder) in the same year "saw for the first time, one of those herds of horses which the Osinipoilles possess in number."[15] He also saw the Assiniboine hunt buffalo using a wooden pound[16] rather than the surround on foot described by Kelsey. While it is evident that some Assiniboine were trading for horses and taking up local residence, others were still taking furs back to the Bay shores.[17]

It has been established, through evidence provided by Cocking, that some Cree were trading horses from the Blackfoot by 1770. Because Blackfoot-Cree trading relations pre-date that time by many years, stretching back at least to 1722, and because the Blackfoot had acquired horses and began trading them to the Assiniboine at least prior to 1754, it is probable that the Cree as well began to receive horses some time between 1732 and 1754. This means that a Cree pattern, similar to that described above for the Assiniboine, likely emerged during the same period. Two groups would have evolved from the original Saskatchewan River Cree – one owning horses and one still relying on canoes. How interrelated these groups were is a matter for speculation.

In summary, it is reasonable to suggest the following conclusions. The Cree trend toward a permanent plains-associated way of life began well before the construction of fur posts on the Saskatchewan River. The acquisition of horses, the maintenance of them and of the means to reach the Bay was a pattern practised by Cree and Assiniboine people. All of them – those who used canoes and those who used horses – were still fur traders in the traditional sense; that is, they traded beaver pelts. The emergence of this dual pattern can be safely placed in the period between 1732 and 1754.

Probably by 1754 and certainly by 1770, some Saskatchewan River Cree had taken on at least one prominent plains trait – horse ownership. But further changes had to be experienced before a clearly identifiable new plains group could emerge and be noted by local traders. This new Cree group would not only own horses but would have a different relationship to the buffalo herds and to the Europeans. They would no longer be the Saskatchewan River Cree of the seventeenth and early eighteenth centuries; they would be Plains Cree.

becoming Plains cree.

These further changes were related to the building of posts on the banks of the Saskatchewan and other plains rivers. The creation of an inland fur-post system accelerated horse ownership by reducing the importance of the canoe. Furthermore, an inland and, most important, an expanded post system gave the Cree and others more economic opportunities in the area of the production of provisions, and brought them to view the herds in a new light. Fortunately, the increased number of whites inland (and thus trade journals) means that the consequences for the Cree of the expansion of the European trade system are relatively well documented.

William McGillivray, in his *Sketches of the Fur Trade* (1809), presents a fur trader's typical assessment of the Indians: "With respect to the Fur Trade, whatever peculiarities each tribe of Indians may have, . . . they are divided by the North West Company into two classes: those who have furs and those who have none, or, the Indians of the mountaineous and woody regions and those of the Plains."/He then expanded his description of both groups. Of the plains tribes he wrote: "The principal aid given by these Indians to the Fur Trader is to kill Buffalo and Deer, and prepare the flesh and tallow for the Company's servants who without this provision, which could not be obtained in any other part of the Country, would be compelled to abandon the most lucrative part of the trade."[18]

increasing inland trade + the start of provision trade (pemmican)

/After 1774, by which time European traders had penetrated the Saskatchewan River area, the fur trade placed a new demand upon the native people of the region. Previously, traders wanted only the most valuable furs, especially the beaver, but now they needed a constant supply of nourishing, portable food to support their increasingly far-reaching enterprise. Prairie buffalo herds were soon recognized as a rich resource./Hunting buffalo to sell dried meat and fat to the posts became an alternative to the trade in furs. Without these provisions, the fur traders would have had to abandon their inland operations. |

The first useful question to be raised within the context of this new situation is: When did the Cree in the area of these new posts turn from beaver hunting to the production of provisions? The second question relates to motivation rather than timing: Were they forced into producing provisions, and thus into a new economic relationship with the traders and the herds, because the beaver resources in their area were depleted? Answering these questions promises an outline of the final stages of the switch from forest to plain.

Initially, the building of inland posts on the eastern section of the Saskatchewan River did not markedly change the situation with respect to the Indians who visited the traders. Mitchell Oman, an HBC trader, explained that it was only when posts had been built "350 miles above Cumberland House" that the traders were finally freed "from being wholly among the Nahathaways and allowed the Indians of the Plains to trade with us."[19] Of course, the Assiniboine, always Cree allies, still came to the eastern Saskatchewan River posts and they did so instead of going to York Factory.[20]

As early as 1781 some Indians were becoming increasingly interested in applying their efforts solely to hunting buffalo. Throughout the following twenty years, they employed an unusual technique to improve their returns. Robert Longmoor drew the Company's attention to it: "The Grounds is all Burnt & no Buffalo, the Natives burnt it, as they was nigh here in the Fall, and far from Beaver Country, on purpose that they might get a great price for provisions." This tactic probably worked well. With each new post the demand for provisions increased. Yet, the Saskatchewan River Cree seem to have remained in the beaver trade. Longmoor assured William Tomison that he had all the Cree "away at Beaver Hunting."[21]

In the next decade, however, during the 1790s, the transition from beaver to buffalo, from forest to plain, was completed. The trade partners of the Cree, the Blackfoot, who prior to 1774 had hunted beaver, wolves and foxes to buy firearms from Cree-Assiniboine traders, were the first to devote themselves almost exclusively to buffalo. By 1793 Tomison characterized them thus: "Of all the different Tribes these are the most indolent in procuring furs." Many Assiniboine bands also began to bring "nothing but buffalo skins." The Cree began to exhibit similar behaviour. On 11 December 1794, the Grand Souteau, a Cree chief, arrived at Fort George (near Manchester House on the North Branch, approximately forty miles above Battleford). Duncan McGillivray learned that "his nation amuse themselves driving Buffalo into a Pound." In the spring of 1795, he noted that the "Crees are quite pitiful this spring having amused themselves during the winter with smoking and feasting along with the Piegans."[22]

There is the possibility that this change in the hunting habits of the Cree was the result of a rapidly disappearing beaver resource. Duncan McGillivray wrote in 1795 that "the Country around Fort George is now entirely ruined. The Natives have already killed all the Beaver to such a distance that they lose much time in coming to the House, during the Hunting Season."[23] In 1797 HBC employee James Bird reported on the state of the beaver resource on the South Branch of the Saskatchewan. He commented, "A great part of the Indians are already in the plains and declare they have not been able to find Beaver."[24]

In view of this development, both the HBC and the Canadian traders moved their posts further west along the North Branch. In 1795, the Canadians built Fort Augustus and the HBC constructed Edmonton House close to it. McGillivray described this area "as a rich and plentiful Country abounding with all kinds of animals especially Beaver and Otters."[25]

The general strategy was not only to get close to richer beaver resources but to divide the Indians. "The lower Fort [Fort George] will only therefore serve in future for the Gens du Large, whilst the Crees, Assiniboine, and Circes, being the Principal Beaver Hunters will resort to [the area of Forts Augustus and Edmonton]."[26] If the Cree could be moved upstream and into contact with an ample supply of beaver, possibly they would stop spending their winters smoking, feasting and pounding buffalo with the Blackfoot.

Other measures to counteract the drift away from beaver hunting had already been taken. Indians who arrived to trade with nothing but provisions were "coldly received" and "treated with less liberality"[27] than Indians who brought in beaver. But the competition between the British and Canadian traders would have blunted the effectiveness of this tactic. The traders were well aware that an Indian badly treated one day might go to the competition with valuable furs the next.

Within three years of the opening of Forts Edmonton and Augustus, the traders realized that their attempt to lure the Cree and others back into beaver hunting and to hold other Cree in that system had failed. James Bird reported to his superior: "I am sorry to inform you that we are utterly disappointed in our hopes that building here near the beaver ground would occasion the Indians hunting Beaver . . . all without exception are tenting in the plains killing Buffalo for themselves to eat."[28] Beaver were still abundant, but the Cree had chosen to opt out of the peltry trade and to become fully involved in buffalo hunting.

To the Canadians this may not have been much of a surprise. They anticipated this drift away from beaver hunting and had taken steps as early as 1794 to compensate for it. In the face of the defection of their "Principal Beaver Hunters"[29] and as a move to make themselves more competitive, the Canadians induced Indians from Lake Superior and Rainy Lake, Indians who were "then Industerious,"[30] to come to the Saskatchewan and hunt beaver. William Tomison at Edmonton House recorded in 1795 that "seven Michelemaccana [Ojibwa] Indians arrived in a canoe . . . these with many more came to the Red River last autumn with the New Company of adventurers."[31] In the same year they were active in the Far West.[32] James Bird's report indicating the failure of the plan to lure the Indians back to beaver hunting noted one bright spot – that the Bungees were still hunting beaver.[33] The Bungees, along with the Swampy Ground Assiniboine and a small group of Strongwood Cree (northern Woodland Cree), were all that were left of the beaver hunters.

The once energetic Saskatchewan River Cree, who for over a hundred years travelled the great distances between York Fort and the plains, had become, in the view of one trader, "a useless sett of lazy indolent fellows a mear nuisance to us;- ... they are generally to be found in large Camps, Winter and Summer, where they remain Idle throughout the year. Buffalo is the only object they have in view."[34]

The long and gradual transition to a plains way of life had begun some time prior to the building of the Saskatchewan River posts; the introduction of horses played an early part in the process. However, given the entrepreneurial tradition of the Saskatchewan River Cree, the increase in the number of traders along the Saskatchewan, as well as the consequent increase in demand for provisions which made buffalo hunting a useful economic undertaking, may have been more critical. Whatever the exact mix of causes was and however individuals and groups reacted to the causes, the transition from the old to the new way of life, and with it the emergence of a Plains Cree people, was made in the 1790s.

In explaining the motivation of the Saskatchewan River Cree, one point cannot be stressed too much. When the Cree changed from beaver to buffalo hunting, there was still an adequate beaver resource which allowed them to continue the profitable trading of prime furs. Therefore, they had alternatives, and they made a choice between one type of hunting and another. They were not pushed out onto the plains "with the exhaustion of woodland food and fur supply," as Oscar Lewis once suggested.[35]

Given the fact that they had an adequate beaver resource, and that after 1774 the resource was close to the suppliers of European goods, making the horse a viable transport method within the old prime fur system, why did the Saskatchewan Cree voluntarily opt out of beaver hunting? The reason may have nothing to do with trade policies or European supplies. Duncan McGillivray identified the cause in 1794 when he described the Plains Indians:

The Inhabitants of the Plains are so advantageously situated that they could live very happily independent of our assistance. They are surrounded with innumerable herds of various kinds of animals, whose flesh affords them excellent nourishment and whose skins defend them from the inclemency of the weather, and they have invented so many methods for the destruction of animals, that they stand in no need of ammunition to provide a sufficiency for these purposes.[36]

The pleasure of living in large groups in the winter and summer, the year-round social activities of the band, and the vast buffalo herds to support this life cannot be discounted as an important cause of the Cree adoption of a plains lifestyle.

One further factor must be considered. A period of diplomatic realignment accompanied the social transformation because the Cree had to relate to old allies on a new basis. They were no longer Saskatchewan River Cree, who were canoe-reliant and were valued trading partners and middlemen to distant Europeans; they

- social life of the groups as important reason for Cree decision to change lifeways.

- alliance w/ Blackfoot ended as they became competitors rather than trading partners were now competitors for plains territory and resources. The central military and trade system of the Saskatchewan River area, the Cree-Blackfoot alliance, could not remain unaffected by the changes of the 1790s. As it evolved, realignment did occur at the turn of the century. One consequence was the end of the Cree-Blackfoot alliance.

Realignment:
The Breakdown of the Cree-Blackfoot Alliance

3

- European weapons became available for all tribes.

The period between 1790 and 1810 is one of considerable complexity in the history of the Plains Cree. It was a time of political instability on the western plains – the adjustment period between an old era and a new one. From a military point of view, the old era had been marked by an imbalance, because gun supplies had reached only some of the western Indians. In this new era, European weapons were available to all tribes. For the Cree, who were becoming residents of the plains, this period of adjustment meant the disappearance of their trading system. Their supply of European articles had always been secure and continued to be so, but as a plains tribe they had to give serious consideration to acquiring horses. The most important change, however, for the Cree, and for the pattern of trade and military activity in the nineteenth century, was the disintegration of their alliance with the Blackfoot.

The Cree-Blackfoot alliance seems to have been peaceful until 1787, when the first notable rupture occurred, and this was only temporary. In June of that year, for reasons unknown, some Cree near Manchester House attacked the "Blood Indians and killed some women and children." As the news spread, "all the Cree Indians fled for the woods for fear of the Blood Indians." What began to look like an all-out war was, however, peacefully settled by the intervention of the Piegan. On 24 August 1787, a small group of Piegan arrived at Manchester House. William Tomison, master at that House, learned that "their chief business [was] to make it up between the Blood Indians and Crees, . . . to be at peace and all to come to the Houses as before." This was an astute diplomatic move. Manchester House was at that time the post farthest west on the North Branch. If the war continued, the Piegan realized, as did the traders, that "it [the war] will do a great deal of harm to this House [Manchester] as the Blood Indians and Muddy River Indians [Piegan] will be afraid to come in."[1] The Cree in 1787 evidently still had the power to close off the supply of European goods to the Blackfoot.

These Piegan departed for their peace mission in the autumn of 1787, taking tobacco as an aid to their discussions.[2] Unfortunately, there are no reports of the success of their conciliatory efforts in that year. But HBC journals state that in 1792 at Manchester House, "one tent of blood Indians . . . has staid to await the arrival of some Nehethewea [Cree] Indians to know whether they intend to keep peace with them or not."[3]

The path of Cree-Blackfoot relations ran smoothly until the early 1790s. Then warfare on the plains became widespread, even sweeping up the traders in its course. The seeds of this disruption were contained in the Cree-Gros Ventre hostility. The western military campaigns of the Cree in the seventeenth and in the first three-quarters of the eighteenth century had been directed against the Snake, Kootenay, Flathead and the Gros Ventre-Naywattame (or Fall) Indians. The Fall Indians, located on the South Branch, had also been involved in the efforts to clear the plains of the Snake and their allies. William Tomison, in the autumn of 1782, reported the return of a war party of Gros Ventre from an expedition against the Snake.[4] As late as 1801, "one hundred Fall Indians set off to War against the Snake Indians"[5] from Chesterfield House on the South Branch of the Saskatchewan. There is no evidence, though, that these Gros Ventre expeditions, although directed against enemies of the Cree and Assiniboine, were assisted by the latter two tribes. On the contrary, their relations seem to have been always violent. The Cree and Assiniboine were at war with the Gros Ventre in 1751, and according to the next available piece of evidence, a 1788 report, they were also engaged in a general war at that time.[6]

Between 1788 and 1793, Cree and Assiniboine attacks on the Gros Ventre continued and seemed to have grown in intensity.[7] In 1793 the Cree struck again, and they struck hard. In the spring a band of Gros Ventre were camped on the banks of the South Branch of the Saskatchewan. They were discovered by a combined force of South Branch and Swan River Cree and some Assiniboine warriors.[8] These Indians "immediately resolved to revenge all their former injuries, by exterminating entirely these unfortunate wretches. . . . They fell upon them like hungry Wolves and with remorseless fury butchered them all in cold blood except for a few children they preserved for Slaves."[9] It was subsequently reported at Buckingham House that two old men had been killed along with one hundred and fifty women and children.[10] This attack filled the Gros Ventre with terror and they fled.[11] The Cree, fearing an equally stunning reprisal, kept on their guard.[12] They waited all summer while the Gros Ventre planned their next move. When it finally came, it was in a most unexpected form.

- continued/increased warfare w/ Gros Ventre.

In the second week of October 1793, a Gros Ventre warrior arrived at Manchester House. He came for tobacco for a party of Gros Ventre led by L'Homme a Calumet,[13] whom, he said, would be there to trade in a few days.[14] On 22 October a Company employee reached Buckingham House with surprising news. William Tomison entered the report in his post journal: "At noon Robert Linklatter arrived and brought the disagreeable News of Manchester House being Robbed of everything belonging to the Company & the Men stripped of everything they possessed, by a body of Fall Indians who came to the House on pretence to trade. . . . They began on the Canadians first [Pine Island Fort] and took a number of Horses & stripped many of their Men. Suppose they were 40 in Number."[15] Duncan McGillivray claimed that this attack on Pine Island Fort was largely unsuccessful – only a few men had lost their personal baggage. He further stated that the Indians' small victory "was bought by the blood of four Savages who afterwards died of the wounds they received on this occasion."[16]

The differences in the reports are secondary to the fact that the Gros Ventre had made such a radical move. Attacking both suppliers of European goods would have seemed sheer madness to all the other Indians. Their decision to do so is a good indication of their desperation.

It is reasonable to assume that if they had been able to avenge themselves directly on the Cree for the spring massacre, the Gros Ventre would have done so. Edward Umfreville in 1790 made a revealing comment on the Gros Ventre when he noted that they "seem not yet to be initiated into the manner of hunting beavers, . . . for they bring nothing to us but wolves."[17] Given the fact that the Cree excluded them from their trade system and that the territory along the South Branch was poor in beaver,[18] the Gros Ventre must have had a very small stock of firearms. Compared to the well-armed, beaver-hunting Cree, they were too weak to force a conclusion. The traders, who, on Duncan McGillivray's evidence the Gros Ventre believed to be "the allies of their enemies,"[19] were safer to attack. Whether or not the Gros Ventre blamed the traders, it was clear to them that an attack on Company posts would be a short cut to acquiring firearms and with firearms they would be on an equal footing with the Cree.

The Gros Ventre, having plundered the traders once, struck again, this time on the South Branch of the Saskatchewan River. On 24 June 1794, two hundred Gros Ventre warriors under the direction of their "War Chief L'Homme de Calumet"[20] attacked the HBC post named South Branch House.[21] After a short fight they captured the post, pillaged it and burnt it to the ground.[22] Magnus Twatt, assigned to the command of Cumberland House for that year, reported the more tragic details: "They likewise killed three of Your Honors Servants the Names of which are Mag. Annel [the trader in charge] William Fea & Hugh Brough [two other men, James

Gaddy and W. Van Driel, escaped] which they cut up in the cruelest manner Immaginable."[23] Then they turned their attention to the North West Company post "which stood only a couple of hundred Rods from the others." The traders there, headed by Louis Chastellain, exhibited "spirited behavior in their enterprize." It is important to note that the traders received "the assistance of several Southward [Cree] Indians."[24]

After the attack on South Branch House, the Cree took up the offensive against the Gros Ventre. In the fall of 1794, they formed a war party, possibly under the direction of The Gauche, a well-known chief of that area, to attack "the Blackfoot."[25] On 7 January 1795 James Bird discovered that the Cree from the Swan River district were assembling to launch a campaign against the Gros Ventre.[26] During the winter of 1794–95, though, the Cree and Blackfoot in that area must have reached a new accord, for that spring they hunted buffalo together.[27]

The Blackfoot had not remained entirely aloof from these battles among the Cree, the traders and the Gros Ventre. They had an interest in good relations with the Cree and the traders, but they also had an established association with the Gros Ventre. The foundation upon which Blackfoot–Gros Ventre relations was based is apparently not recorded until the early 1800s, when the Gros Ventre, who had maintained earlier ties with the Arapaho, their closest Algonkian-speaking relations, became a vital link between the Blackfoot and the Arapaho-Cheyenne horse market south of the Missouri. Maintaining friendly relations with both the Gros Ventre and Cree would prove an increasingly difficult task for the Blackfoot.

If the turmoil of 1793–94 demonstrates anything other than the Gros Ventre's desperate need of weapons, it indicates that the Blackfoot were being forced to consider an exclusive alliance with either the Gros Ventre or the Cree. It also shows that the Cree were determined to oppose the Gros Ventre, even at the cost of their Blackfoot alliance, and were dedicated to the protection of their source of strength.

After the summer of 1794 the Gros Ventre were reported to have withdrawn toward the southwest.[28] The Blackfoot covered their retreat with a diplomatic explanation: the guilty Gros Ventre, who were only a part of that nation, had formed an alliance with the Snake.[29] The truth of the matter was that they had gone to visit the Arapaho.[30]

Cree campaigns between 1795 and 1800 were directed exclusively against the Snake, Kootenay and Flathead. Then in the fall of 1800 a large band of Blackfoot "near killed 3 Southard [Cree] Indians . . . but luckily they made their escape after the above Indians had got intoxicated."[31] With these preliminaries barely under way, the Gros Ventre made an appearance. Again they were in a desperate mood and again they focussed their frustrations on the traders. On 8 March 1802, A Kas Kin, a leading Gros Ventre chief, along with a band of warriors, approached

Chesterfield House (the HBC post which replaced South Branch House). Peter Fidler, the trader in charge, though he managed to defuse the immediate danger, learned subsequently that the Gros Ventre had returned to the Missouri to recruit a war party from among the Arapaho and had planned to attack the Company, the Cree and the Assiniboine.[32]

The warfare, which the Cree had initiated in the spring of 1793 by their massacre of the Gros Ventre, came to a temporary halt in 1803 when a party of Cree and Assiniboine renewed their peace with the Blackfoot.[33] This peace lasted until the summer of 1806. Then, James Bird, at Edmonton, noted: "A fatal Quarrel has taken place between the Blackfeet and Southern Indians; . . . a battle had been fought between them in which 28 of the former, and three of the latter had fallen.- . . . The Southern Indians are flying in all Quarters. . . . How far the effects of this Quarrel may extend is impossible to foresee."[34] The battle was followed by an ambush and killing of four tents of Cree Indians returning from a visit to the Piegan.[35] The result of these troubles was the dissolution of the Cree-Blackfoot alliance. The diplomatic link which had been worn thin by the turmoil of the 1790s finally snapped in 1806. *1806*

Although the immediate cause of the battles of 1806 is unknown, the outcome of the only recorded Cree-Blackfoot joint campaign against the Gros Ventre reveals one of the underlying currents that caused the final disruption. D.W. Harmon recorded the story in his journal: "Six Assiniboines arrived and inform us that about Eighty Lodges of Crees and Assiniboins with about as many Blackfoot were on their way to wage war on the Rapid [Gros Ventre] Indians but the . . . tribes fell out on the way respecting a horse which they both claimed, and which neither could relinquish and fought a battle amongst themselves."[36] A number of factors, including the Cree-Assiniboine problems acquiring horses, caused the final rupture. Over this period the Cree were going out onto the plains in increasingly large numbers and needed horses. Their abandonment of beaver trapping in the mid-1790s reduced their wealth and consequently their ability to purchase horses. Alexander Henry (the Younger) observed this when he wrote of the Plains Cree: "Indolence and gluttony seems to be their sole object. In the winter season they take the Bow and Arrow. Firearms are scarce among them. . . . If they can procure a gun they instantly give it to the Assiniboines in exchange for a horse."[37] Their campaigns against the Gros Ventre were undoubtedly designed, in part, to supplement their poor stock of horses. As early as 1801 some Arapaho, conducted by the Gros Ventre, visited the South Branch area.[38] By 1807 a connection had been made between the Arapaho, Cheyenne and Blackfoot through which the latter began to receive horses.[39] Had the Cree made peace with the Gros Ventre, they too could have entered

- warfare for acquisition of horses.

the Arapaho-Cheyenne horse market. By continuing their campaigns, they forced the Blackfoot to side with the Gros Ventre and their southern supply of horses.

Throughout the eighteenth century the Cree had been a valuable source of weapons for the Blackfoot. Even as late as 1787 the Piegan had been careful to keep peace between their nation and the Cree so that the flow of European goods could continue. The Blackfoot alliance with the Gros Ventre was not in those years an important economic asset for the Blackfoot, so they could afford to avert their eyes from Cree depredations. The opening of Edmonton House in 1795 and Rocky Mountain House in 1799[40] changed this situation. The Blackfoot then had direct and secure access to European goods within their own territory. As the economic importance of the Cree alliance declined and the benefits of a Gros Ventre alliance increased, the matter became quite simple for the Blackfoot. They no longer needed the Cree to get firearms and they had acquired a secure supply of horses through the Gros Ventre; the Cree were therefore expendable. The alliance was ended by the Blackfoot in 1806. The Cree attitude of implacable hostility to the Gros Ventre undoubtedly pushed the Blackfoot into that decision.

The problem set for the Cree by the breakdown of the Blackfoot alliance was more than military. They did, of course, launch war parties directly against their new enemy. They also worked to isolate the Blackfoot from white traders. In 1808 they tried the same tactics of blockade that the Blackfoot had used against the Kootenay, Flathead and Snake. Alexander Henry (the Younger), on his way up the Saskatchewan, was informed: "[The] Crees . . . had assembled at the Battle River and had determined to prevent us from passing upwards to keep the Slave [Blackfoot] Indians from receiving any supplies from us in arms and ammunition."[41] This move was no more successful for the Cree than it was for the Blackfoot, and it appears not to have been repeated. Apart from the fact that the Cree could hardly afford to increase the number of their enemies by opposing the traders, a blockade would not solve a more serious logistical problem; the Cree had lost their source of horses by going to war with the Gros Ventre and Blackfoot. They could not expect to prosper, either in war or in life on the plains, without finding a new source. Some time between 1806 and 1810 they made contact with the Flathead and began to supply them with guns and ammunition. In the new military pattern which the Cree had to form, a central consideration would be the acquisition of a reliable supply of horses; the only possible solution here was a military alliance with a horse-trading tribe against the Blackfoot.

Fortunately, the Cree did have opportunities other than a Flathead alliance that could provide easy acquisition of horses. The evolution of Plains Cree culture was not restricted to the area around the Saskatchewan River. The Cree had also exploited the Red River drainage basin and played the roles of trade partner and military ally in that district. It was possible, in theory at least, that the social transformation, the adoption of a plains way of life by Red River Cree, and the resulting realignment of their eighteenth-century military-trade system would not have separated them from their traditional and horse-rich allies in this area, the Mandan-Hidatsa.

- Cree acquisition of horses for increased warfare with Blackfoot & continued life on the plains was provided by the Mandan-Hidatsa trade system.

THE CREE AND THE
MANDAN-HIDATSA TRADERS

II

Overleaf: Plains Cree driving buffalo into pound (Glenbow Archives, Calgary, NA-1406-101)

Military Patterns on the Southeastern Plains, 1730 to 1805

4

The area of the southeastern plains has been portrayed as the homestead of the Selkirk settlers, the base camp of both the colourful Métis buffalo hunters and eager missionaries dreaming of rich harvests in native souls, the battleground of Canada's one successful rebellion, and the origin of the province of Manitoba. On the part of fur-trade historians, these preoccupations are understandable. Yet, in the shadows of the fur trade and struggling prairie settlement, significant events were occurring in the course of Indian history and, in particular, Cree history.

The Mandan-Hidatsa trading centre and Cree participation in it are probably the most important factors in the history of the Plains Cree on the southeastern plains. *pre existing* This centre must represent a high point in plains economic organization. It was the *European* home of a native trade system which was in existence prior to the European fur *fur trade* trade and then adapted well to the introduction of European goods. The Cree and their Assiniboine allies had an important role in its operation, both as traders supplying European goods and as military actors in the area. As in the Northwest with regard to the Cree-Blackfoot trade system, here again military, diplomatic and economic factors were linked from the early eighteenth century onward.

The most western of Woodland Cree people, prior to the trade era, inhabited the banks of the Winnipeg River. There, some time in the seventeenth century, they welcomed the Assiniboine, originally of the Sioux nation. Jointly, the Cree and the Assiniboine entered the Hudson's Bay Company trade system and became familiar with the territory west of Lake Winnipeg. However, this northern and western involvement did not immediately cause them to relinquish their homeland nor their involvement in the inter-tribal politics of that area. The Cree-Assiniboine maintained a stake in this eastern area well into the eighteenth century and, in a southern and western extension, they were prime powers throughout the trade era. /

Documentary evidence for the military and trade activities of these Cree appears relatively late. Although there are many references to the Cree north of Lake Superior and along the shores of Hudson Bay,[1] references to the Winnipeg River Cree are not made until 1730. Pierre Gaultier, Sieur de la Vérendrye, reported to Beauharnois on 10 October 1730 the content of a conversation with Poko and Petit Jour, two Cree chiefs from Lake Nipigon.[2] They informed him of their move westward and provided him with a description of the tribes of that area, the Cree, the Assiniboine and the Sioux.[3] As La Vérendrye himself moved west and established his chain of fur posts, he acquired more detailed firsthand information on the country west of Rainy Lake. In 1749, the year before his death, he summarized this knowledge in a short memorandum.[4] In it he disclosed the deployment of the Cree and Assiniboine tribes. The territory around Lake of the Woods was held by the Cree and their Monsoni allies. At the mouth of the Winnipeg River, where he had built Fort Maurepas, lived the Cree of the Bois-fort. To the northwest of Fort Maurepas, in the area of Cedar Lake and Lake Winnipegosis, were the Cree of the Lakes and Little Rivers, and the Cree of the Prairies and the Canoe Assiniboine. The Assiniboine were also on the banks of the Assiniboine River.[5] Although it is not mentioned in his memorandum of 1749, he did note in earlier reports that Cree lived around the mouth of the Red River and on the Assiniboine at least as far along as the Forks.[6]

In conversations with visiting chiefs, both Cree and Assiniboine, he recorded important information relating to existing military patterns; he found that the Sioux and Saulteaux waged war against the Monsoni, Cree and Assiniboine.[7] This was a continuing pattern too firmly established for La Vérendrye to change. His mission to discover the western sea depended on the Cree. Fort Charles, built in 1733 as the first French fort in Cree territory, was not the Indians' only source of European goods. The Cree of Lake Winnipeg and Red River were undoubtedly already using the well-known routes north to the English traders at Hudson Bay, and the Assiniboine in the Assiniboine River area employed Lake Manitoba for the same purpose.[8] The Cree, with an alternate northern source of trade goods and control of La Vérendrye's intended westward route, forced him into their mould. A.S. Morton's picture of the romantic, battle-scarred, trader-explorer standing in council with the Cree, asserting "his ascendancy over his dusky subjects,"[9] smoothing the way for his expansion west, and "preventing them from raiding tribes Friendly to the French, . . ."[10] seems to have no foundation in reality. E.E. Rich came much closer to revealing the situation. He noted that La Vérendrye's "dependence on them grew to such an extent that in 1734 he sanctioned their adoption of his eldest son, to go on the war path with them against the Sioux."[11] Morton himself admits that in the end La Vérendrye could not convince the Cree to stop their warfare on the Sioux of the plains.[12]

This failure and La Vérendrye's subsequent support of continued Cree campaigns in the early 1730s led to personal tragedy. In June 1736 the Sioux struck back against the French-Cree-Assiniboine. They ambushed a party of twenty-one French led by La Vérendrye's eldest son, Jean-Baptiste, and killed them all.[13] Like true allies the Cree immediately came to La Vérendrye's aid. "On the twenty sixth [June] four canoes and twelve men arrived Cree and Assiniboin from the neighbourhood of Lake Winnipeg, the two tribes having assembled at fort Maurepas to beg me earnestly to let them know if I intended to go and avenge the Blood of the French, and particularly that of my son."[14] These Cree and Assiniboine left Fort Maurepas and travelled to the Red River some distance above its junction with the Assiniboine, "which was the usual rendezvous for Assiniboine, Cree, Monsoni . . . in order to reach the Sioux."[15] When all the warriors had congregated at the meeting place their number reached eight hundred. This was not the only retaliatory attack that was launched. La Colle, a Monsoni chief, told La Vérendrye that he also had organized a party of three hundred warriors, including Cree, Assiniboine and Monsoni.[16] Throughout the second half of the 1730s and beyond, La Colle and his Cree-Assiniboine warriors launched campaigns against the Sioux in the eastern part of the Winnipeg–Rainy River waterway. As late as the autumn of 1742, La Colle, whose territory was around Rainy Lake, gathered together two hundred men, mostly Cree and Assiniboine, and struck a hard blow at the Sioux.[17]

In this southeastern area the Cree also contacted the Mandan-Hidatsa.[18] These Siouan-speaking, village-dwelling agriculturalists lived just downstream from the Big Bend where the Missouri River turns sharply south. La Vérendrye's comments on Cree-Mandan-Hidatsa relations appear in separate journal entries of 1733. He noted that in the past, "Cree and Assiniboine have constantly made war upon them and have captured several children from them," and then that the "Cree and Assiniboine have made peace with that Tribe."[19]

The attractiveness for the Cree of a Mandan-Hidatsa peace was twofold. The first element was revealed in a further entry in 1733. La Vérendrye reported that the Indians "were leaving in the spring to go to the Ouachipouennes (Mandans) in order to buy corn from them."[20] Corn was an ideal, portable food supply for winter hunting expeditions and for the long-distance travel that Cree and Assiniboine middlemen were involved in. It, like pemmican, was an important tool in the prosecution of the native fur trade.

The second element, a further possible cause for a link between these people, was their mutual enmity for the Sioux. The Sioux had forced the Mandan on a number of occasions, before 1730, to abandon their villages and move to new sites.[21]

These factors – the value of corn, the common enemy and, in addition, the value of the Cree-Assiniboine as owners and eventually merchants of European weapons – would have been the three legs of the tripod upon which the peace of 1733 and, perhaps, subsequent military cooperation rested. La Vérendrye's nephew's notation in 1735 certainly points in that direction: "The Assiniboine added that they were going to start with their families and go to the Ouachipouennes and would leave their families with them while they went to make war in another quarter."[22] Mandan-Hidatsa billets and armed Cree-Assiniboine warriors would have added significantly to the ability of all to withstand Sioux aggression. The Mandan-Hidatsa villages would be an ideal domicile for Cree-Assiniboine women and children. While the warriors took to the field, their families would help produce the agricultural products which made the villages the hub of trade.

This Cree-Assiniboine–Mandan-Hidatsa peace did not cause the Sioux to abandon their campaigns, of course. The peace had to become an alliance and the alliance had to be more than a threat based on the consolidation of power. It had to be active in a military way. The Sioux were relentless, their raiders extended their war trips up into the Assiniboine River area as well as to village sites on the Missouri. In 1738 La Vérendrye, on his way to visit the villages, was told by some Assiniboine that the "Sioux often visit in that direction and I had need of an escort."[23] The Assiniboine kept in constant contact with the villages in this period. They informed the Mandan-Hidatsa of La Vérendrye's intention to visit them and, when La Vérendrye met a Mandan chief, the chief spoke Assiniboine.

Unfortunately, when La Vérendrye withdrew from the southeastern plains, the course of Mandan-Hidatsa, Assiniboine and Cree relations receded into obscurity until late in the eighteenth century. Hostilities between the Mandan and Hidatsa indicated that their relationship, at least, had periods of instability. Indeed at one point the Sioux and Mandan attempted an alliance. At a Hidatsa village in 1806 Alexander Henry (the Younger) found a pile of human bones, the remains of a Sioux raiding party of 1790. The Sioux had attempted to isolate the Hidatsa by making a peace with the Mandans. This they accomplished, but their siege of the Hidatsa villages had been a failure.[24] How long this Mandan-Sioux peace lasted is not known.

The only positive reference made in existing evidence to relations between the Cree, Assiniboine and Sioux in this dark period is the tradition of a great Sioux victory near Lake Winnipeg. Both Alexander Henry (the Younger)[25] and John McDonnell, another trader, present a recollection which has its roots in the origin of the name Rivière aux Morts. McDonnell wrote: "Three leagues from the lake, the River aux morts enters the Red River on the north side. Here a large camp of Assiniboils, Cree and Sauteux were massacred by the Sioux or Naudawesis, the most powerful nation in all the interior country. Ever since this slaughter, the river has been called with propriety, Rivière aux morts."[26] It was David Thompson's understanding that Cree-Assiniboine-Sioux warfare had been continuous. In a recapitulation of events from the Assiniboine-Sioux division until the year 1812, he refers to this unceasing enmity and the success of the Assiniboine who, "with the Nahathaways, who accompanied them to war were powerful, and with their allies, made their brethren the Sioux Nation feel the Weight of their resentment for several years, until the smallpox of 1782 came, which involved them all in one calamity, and very much reduced the numbers of all parties."[27] Although the epidemic may have lessened the tempo of warfare, it did not stop it, nor did it cause any change in the structure of the military pattern.

Whether the Cree, Assiniboine and Sioux fought continually between 1742 and the 1780s or whether they reached some temporary settlements is a matter of conjecture. It is definite, however, that a state of warfare existed between them in 1793. In that year John McDonnell reported the return of a successful Assiniboine war party which had set out to find the Sioux south of the Missouri.[28] Furthermore, it is noteworthy that in 1797 "the Mandales, Cristineaux and Assiniboils have combined together and engaged in war with the Panies [Pawnees or Arikara] . . . and fought a Battle this summer."[29]

Thus by 1800 the pattern of Cree-Assiniboine-Mandan friendliness and cooperation, which was first noticed in the 1730s by La Vérendrye, is again clearly discernible. In March 1800 messengers circulated among the Cree and Assiniboine camps, bringing the news that the Sioux were prowling in the area of the villages. War parties were subsequently dispatched and in the autumn they returned with the joyous news that they had "fought a great battle with some Sioux's & got the advantage of them, they sang and danced ye whole night."[30] In the spring a joint Assiniboine, Cree, Ojibwa and Mandan force was assembled.[31] However, almost as quickly as the Cree-Assiniboine–Mandan-Hidatsa relationship showed signs of stability in the 1790s, it began to falter. In a series of cryptic entries in the Brandon House journal beginning on 20 December 1801, the course of a Mandan-Assiniboine crisis is summarized. On 20 December 1801 the Mandans killed eleven Assiniboine.[32] The next spring the Assiniboine were reported to be moving northward to escape Mandan war parties. By November 1808 peace seems to have been restored.[33] Nowhere in this evidence is any cause suggested for these hostilities, nor is the position of the Cree indicated.

Activity in 1804 and 1805 could once again be concentrated on the Sioux. Alexander Henry (the Younger) noted that in the summer of 1804 the Assiniboine-Saulteaux formed two war parties, the second composed of three hundred warriors, and directed their steps toward Sioux country.[34] The following year, 1805, another party of three hundred, including a contingent of Cree warriors, set out to battle the

- continued Cree-Assiniboine warfare w/ Sioux; 1800 alliance w/ M-H was still strong/renewed.

Sioux. The Mandan and Hidatsa, united under the leadership of the False Horn chief, "went to war towards the Sioux country."[35]

This point of accord and unified opposition to the Sioux is an ideal place to halt and to look back at the course of Cree, Assiniboine, Mandan and Hidatsa relations. One preliminary observation can be made immediately. This relationship was quite different from the Cree alliance with the Blackfoot in that its first goal was not the conquest of territory but was, more likely, the preservation of the settlements against aggressors, primarily the Sioux. Cooperative, coordinated military undertakings of the type noted by La Vérendrye's nephew would have been beneficial to all. It may well have been the Cree-Assiniboine, with their direct connection to a source of European weapons, who bolstered the military strength of the Mandan-Hidatsa, protected the settlements and prevented a dispersal of the people. However, even if the Mandan-Hidatsa were the weak partners, they did provide a clear economic benefit to the Cree through the production of agricultural products. In a subtle and much more complex degree than in Cree-Blackfoot relations, Cree-Assiniboine–Mandan-Hidatsa relations were a mix of military and trade interests. It is only by looking at the trade side of the relationship that some sense can be made of the central position of the Mandan-Hidatsa and also of the troubled state of that relationship between 1794 and 1805, and in the years thereafter.

-warfare w/Sioux was of a defensive nature, with Blackfoot was of competition.

Cree Participation in the Mandan-Hidatsa Trade System, 1806 to 1837

[handwritten margin note: — complex, far reaching European post were subsumed parts of a greater system, trascending political level]

5

European goods penetrated the plains prior to the arrival of the white traders. The Blackfoot acquired firearms and iron tools at least twenty years before their first meeting with a white person. The Mandan-Hidatsa were attacked by Sioux warriors wielding European weapons before La Vérendrye reached the villages. By the time white traders finally caught up with the spread of their articles, they were apt to find a functioning trade system interwoven with military alliances, such as Cocking found between the Cree and Blackfoot. The Cree-Blackfoot trade organization, although it was effective in promoting specific military goals, was unsophisticated compared to the Mandan-Hidatsa trade system.

When La Vérendrye visited the Mandan-Hidatsa villages, he entered the grand mart of the plains. The trade tentacles which stretched out fan-like from these villages reached westward to the Pacific coast, to the Spanish settlements in the south, to the shores of Hudson Bay in the north, and at least as far east as Lake of the Woods. In geographic area alone the scope of the trade system rivalled that of the HBC. Considering the fact that the British, French and Canadian merchants traded through it, it can be suggested in all seriousness that for a time the European outlets were a sub-system within the Mandan-Hidatsa trade organization. Like that of the HBC, the Mandan-Hidatsa trade system managed to transcend many political divisions for the sake of trade.

In La Vérendrye's journals and reports covering the years between 1733 and 1749, some light is thrown on part of the structure of the trade system. In those years the Mandan-Hidatsa became connected with a source of European goods and, incidentally, a source which was controlled by Cree-Assiniboine middlemen. They received knives, axes, fire steels and other iron tools, paying for them with their own agricultural produce, mainly corn and beans. La Vérendrye, on the basis of a conversation with an Assiniboine, concluded that "the Assiniboine were the only ones who brought them" European goods.[2] His trip to the villages and the separate visits of his men and sons disclosed, even at this early date, a well-developed system.

The Assiniboine who escorted La Vérendrye to the villages in 1738 travelled slowly, with a definite purpose in mind. The scouts who preceded the column kept a sharp lookout for the Sioux and for buffalo.

Buffalo hunts were conducted en route to supplement the supply of fat and meat that the Assiniboine would trade to the Mandan-Hidatsa "to eat with the grain [corn] of which they always eat much, having seldom either meat or fat."[3] Even La Vérendrye purchased fat at the Assiniboine encampment before they set out.[4]

Arriving at the villages, the French and Assiniboine were greeted by the chief, who presented them with a very appropriate "gift of Indian corn in the ear, and of their Tobacco in rolls." After these cordial preliminaries were completed, business was conducted. The villagers displayed their stores of corn, beans, tobacco, painted feathers, painted buffalo robes, deer skins, dressed buckskin, garters, decorative headbands and girdles. On their part, the Assiniboine offered buffalo meat and fat, kettles, axes, muskets, powder, balls, knives and awls. Unfortunately, there is no information about the rates of exchange. La Vérendrye does note, though, that the Mandan "are cunning traders, cheating the Assiniboines of all they may possess."[5]

The dressed and decorated skins, both buffalo and deer, were acquired by the villagers through trade. Each summer, usually in the month of June, "there arrived at the great fort on the bank of the river of the Mandan, several savage tribes which use horses and carry on trade with them; that they bring dressed skins trimmed and ornamented with plummage and porcupine quills, painted in various colours, also white buffalo-skins, and that the Mandan give them in exchange grain and beans."[6] In the spring of 1739 two hundred tents of these Indians arrived at the villages. They were from different allied tribes, one of which "came from the setting of the sun, where there are white men living in towns and in forts made of bricks and white stone."[7]

In 1741 La Vérendrye's sons, Francois and Louis-Joseph, returned from a trip to the villages where they had hoped to meet the Gens des Chevaux (Horse People) and travel west with them. Failing to make this connection, they returned north and brought with them two horses "and four little tubes [beads] which he says are of porcelain an article much used among the people of the Sea."[8]

The Mandan did conduct Francois and Louis-Joseph southwestward in 1742 and then turned them over to the protection of the Beaux Hommes (Good Men). Finally, after much wandering, they met the Gens des Chevaux. These Indians told them of the ravages of their enemy, the Gens du Serpent (Snake Indians), who cap-

1730s
- agricultural produce at the
  center of trade: European goods, meat/fat products,
  horses

tured young women "and traded them at the sea coast for horses and merchandize."
In a summary comment on their journey, they noted that "all the tribes of that
country have a large number of horses, asses, and mules."[9]

J.C. Ewers, who has made a special study of the horse trade on the plains, suggests that the plains tribes who visited the villages included the Crow, Cheyenne,
Arapaho, Comanche, Kiowa-Apache and Kiowa.[10] From among these tribes, ex-
cluding the Cheyenne and Arapaho, may be found the identification of the Gens
des Chevaux, Bow, Beaux Hommes and of the other Indians who met La
Vérendrye's sons.

The evidence pertaining to the years between 1733 and 1742 discloses certain
interesting characteristics of the Mandan-Hidatsa trade system (see Table 2).

The naturalness of the relationships among the participants of the Mandan-
Hidatsa trade centre is evident. They exchanged goods typical of their divergent
ways of life – it was an exchange of the products of the garden for the products of
the hunt. Clearly, the trading centre, as a focus for these types of relationships, existed for many years before the introduction of European goods. Traditional
economic behaviour was displayed by the participants' production of a surplus for
trade to supplement indigenous products of their own country with products available from other territories. The labour of one group supplemented the labour of the
other.

The inclusion of craft items for trade reveals that the needs being served were
more than those of basic survival.

It is evident that the villages' agricultural products were the common coinage
of the trade system, and that the Mandan-Hidatsa played the central and determining role in the trade. There is no evidence of horses being traded to Indians east of
the villages prior to 1741; nor is there evidence that the Mandan-Hidatsa traded
European goods westward in these early years. La Vérendrye notes that in the conduct of their trade with the Assiniboine the Mandan-Hidatsa made the best deals.
His opinion, though, is undoubtedly based on a French scale of prices, which would
have reserved valuable items such as firearms for the acquisition of prime furs. It
can be suggested that the Mandan-Hidatsa system operated, at least partially, on an
Indian schedule of prices, structured by Indian demands and values, which were
not those of the white traders. The Assiniboine, no doubt, considered the agricultural produce of the Mandan-Hidatsa gardens as very valuable commodities.[11]

During the second half of the eighteenth century, important structural changes
occurred in this trade system. The type of agricultural products traded were still
those that had been traded in the 1730s, but the selection of European goods became more varied as the competition between the HBC and the Canadian companies
escalated. Added to the limited list of La Vérendrye's era were items such as hawk

TABLE 2
Trade in the Mandan-Hidatsa Trade System

Assiniboine (Cree) ⟵⟶	Mandan ⟵⟶	Western Plains Tribes
meat	agricultural products	hides
fat	hides	handicrafts
European goods	handicrafts	horses

bells, small saws, iron lances and brass rings.[12] The embargo on English goods being traded westward by the Mandan-Hidatsa was lifted in the second half of the eighteenth century and these, in conjunction with agricultural products, became the standard medium of exchange to the western tribes. A summary of goods traded through the system in the years between 1790 and 1837 is given in Table 3.

By 1805 the Mandan-Hidatsa were investing most of their agricultural production in trade, holding in reserve only enough to provide a cushion for emergencies such as a Sioux siege. Buffalo meat was substituted for corn and beans as the staple of their diet because their increased ownership of horses now enabled them to hunt buffalo at greater distances from the villages.[13] As their consumption of buffalo increased, their demand for Assiniboine-produced supplies of meat and fat declined. Buffalo robes, which were a by-product of this activity, found their way to the British and Canadian posts.[14]

Liquor was not used by the Mandan either for relaxation or trade, although it can be safely assumed that it was offered to them by the white traders. Handicrafts (painted feathers and robes, and decorated items of clothing, for example) remained an item of trade. Trade in these articles, and in agricultural products, demonstrates the basic stability of the system's design. It was geared to trade in general rather than to the fur trade in particular. A good example of this was the trade in eagle feathers, which were used as decorative items, often with considerable spiritual power, especially for sacred pipes. The tail feathers of two eagles carried the value of a good horse or a gun.[15] Prime furs were traded along with these other commodities, but they were handled no differently from other items.[16]

The Cree and Assiniboine continued to play an important, if changing, part in village trade. Throughout the latter part of the eighteenth century, they were regular suppliers of European goods. In the 1790s the conditions relative to trade with Europeans, which had existed during most of the century, changed. Both the HBC and the Canadian companies built posts along the Assiniboine and Red rivers. This accelerated the adoption of a pattern of a plains way of life similar to that which was taking place on the northern plains at that time. The building of posts in Cree, Assiniboine and Ojibwa territory caused a decrease in the importance of the canoe as the necessity for the trip to Hudson Bay or to Lake Superior disappeared. Al-

TABLE 3
Mandan-Hidatsa Trade System, 1790 to 1837

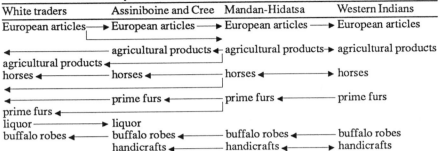

White traders	Assiniboine and Cree	Mandan-Hidatsa	Western Indians
European articles ⟶	European articles ⟶	European articles ⟶	European articles
	agricultural products ⟵	agricultural products ⟶	agricultural products
agricultural products ⟵			
horses ⟵	horses ⟵	horses ⟵	horses
⟵			
	prime furs ⟵	prime furs ⟵	prime furs
prime furs ⟵			
liquor ⟶	liquor		
buffalo robes ⟵	buffalo robes ⟵	buffalo robes ⟵	buffalo robes
	handicrafts ⟵	handicrafts ⟵	handicrafts

though the profitability of hunting buffalo for trade to the Mandan villages declined, the hunt was given new life in Cree territory by the demands of the increasing number of European traders. With the necessity for the long trading trip gone, and the demand of the European traders for provisions ensured, the Cree and Assiniboine became more attracted to a plains way of life, and thus were increasingly interested in owning horses.

The Cree of the southeastern plains would seem to have been in an ideal position to purchase horses. Unlike their northern and western relatives, who were barred from the horse-trading system of that area by their opposition to the Gros Ventre, the southeastern Cree had access to the Mandan-Hidatsa who controlled the major horse mart of the eastern plains. Other factors, however, intervened, factors which undermined the position of the Cree and Assiniboine, limiting their ability to purchase horses, and finally bringing about the collapse of their trade relations with the villages. There is abundant information in traders' journals about the conduct of trade through the Mandan-Hidatsa villages. Unfortunately for the Cree and Assiniboine, the Mandan-Hidatsa controlled the trade strictly.

Evidence pertaining to the years 1804 through 1806 discloses the yearly bustle of activity at the Mandan and Hidatsa villages. In those years the Lewis and Clark expedition visited the villages, as did many HBC and Canadian traders. A few traders left lively and informative records of what they saw. They wrote about the annual spring fair, which was the centre of trade activity. Touring the villages, Alexander Henry (the Younger) noted that "the women [were] all very busy employed taking up their hidden treasures and making preparations for the approaching Fair."[17] When the various tribes had assembled, the trading began in earnest. Henry enthusiastically proclaimed that "it represented a perfect Country Fair. Everyone was

- the cree became interested in plains lifeway & needed horses for that.

anxious to dispose of her property to advantage and for this purpose they carry their load from tent to tent before they can dispose of the whole."[18]

It was a colourful and exciting time. The brightly painted teepees of the plains tribes stood out sharply against the somber wood and mud-covered village houses clustered along the Missouri. Drifting from the teepees and houses were the sharp, chanting rhythms of dancers and singers, the yelping of battling hordes of dogs and the excited cries of the children. When the Cree and Assiniboine visited the villages in 1804, the celebrations continued for two full days.[19]

After the greetings and cordial gift exchanges that were the traditional preliminaries, loud voices could be heard as the plains messengers "[rode] both within and without the Camp at full speed haranguing with great vehemence ordering their own people to receive their friends well, to take them into their Tents secure their property from Theft give them plenty to eat, and in the end to exchange with them their own commodities for those of their relations upon equal terms and not to cheat or wrong anybody of their Property."[20] In spite of their cordiality the villagers must have been amused by the last words in the message to the plains people. The dancing, singing and fine words were really only a thin veneer covering the hard-nosed rates of exchange set by the Mandan-Hidatsa and applied to all who came to trade. The villagers would not allow the good fellowship of the fair sway them from full realization of their profits. Their trade tyranny was nowhere more strikingly displayed than in their trade in European articles and horses.

The Mandan-Hidatsa appreciated the value of European goods and the desire for them on the part of their western trading partners. A prominent Hidatsa chief, Le Borgne, although bewildered by the behaviour of the whites, clearly saw the benefits of it: "White men love beaver and they are continually in search of beaver for its skin. What use they make of the skin I do not know, but they give us good things in return. They exchange it for guns, ammunition etc. Our fathers were not acquainted with white men – we live better than our fathers lived."[21] These Indian traders were not about to let advantages slip through their fingers. Not being beaver hunters themselves, their livelihood depended on keeping the western tribes isolated from sources of European goods. With this as a basic policy, they prevented white traders from going westward beyond the villages. La Roque, a Canadian who planned to explore up the Missouri, had their position fully explained to him. The Mandan asserted that "if the white people would extend their dealings to the Rocky Mountains the Mandans would thereby become great sufferers as they not only would lose all the benefits which they had hitherto derived from their intercourse with these distant tribes but in measure as these tribes obtained arms they would become independent and insolent in the extreme."[22] The fear was not that the western tribes were armed but that they would acquire a source of arms independent

M-H trade system base on inflated rates of exchange;
control of the flux of goods, particularly guns/horses.

of Mandan-Hidatsa control. They were quite willing to trade arms to these Indians. For the sake of profit and security, they wished to keep it that way.

In 1805 Charles McKenzie witnessed a trading session between the Crow Mountain Indians (Crow) and the villagers. He was amazed at "the great quantity of merchandize which the Missouri Indians [had] accumulated by their intercourse with Indians [Cree-Assiniboine] that visit[ed] them from the vicinity of commercial establishments."[23] While smoking the pipe of friendship, the Crow were offered "two hundred guns, with one hundred rounds of ammunition for each, a hundred bushells of Indian corn, a quantity of mercantile articles such as kettles, axes, clothes etc. The Corbeaux in return brought two hundred and fifty horses, large parcels of buffalo robes, leather leggins, shirts etc."[24] Although on the surface this may appear to be an equitable exchange, it was far from that. The Mandan-Hidatsa were in complete control of the business conducted. Alexander Henry, who had been so enthusiastic about the fair, concluded, after viewing a similar trading session, that the Crow were kept "in subjection."[25] The core of his complaint was that the Mandan-Hidatsa set "their own price for their horses and every other [article] they bring nor will they allow a stranger to give the real value of their commodities, the price once fixed by these scoundrels, they will permit you to give no more than they offer themselves. By this means they generally get into their hands the total of whatever is brought into their Villages, and then sell out again to strangers for double what it cost them."[26]

Their control over prices seemed unbreakable. The plains tribes could only submit, and the white traders were in no position to force a change in the trading rules of the villages. The villagers held the whites in no great esteem. When introduced by Charles McKenzie to Chaboillez and Henry, the supervisors of the Canadian traders in that area, the Mandan chiefs told them that "the Great Chiefs in the Spanish Settlements were clothed in dresses that dazzled the eyes of the Indians, that they were surrounded with armed men who had many slaves in attendance, and that they made many presents to the Mandanes. Your Chiefs . . . are white like the Chiefs of the Spaniards, but they are not Great Chiefs, nor do they look like Chiefs." Even the semi-military company of Lewis and Clark was viewed with disdain. One Hidatsa chief expressed the opinion, "Had I these white warriors in the upper plains, . . . my young men on horseback would do for them as they would do for so many wolves . . . for there are only two sensible men among them, the Worker of Iron and the Maker of Guns."[27]

Henry had noted that what the Mandan-Hidatsa received from one tribe of plains Indians they doubled in price before trading to other western tribes or to the Cree and Assiniboine. They applied the same markup to European goods received from the northeast. For one hundred made beaver (MB) Henry purchased "a tolerable

- M-H traded European goods acquired through Cree-Assiniboine. to in the North, for horses from Crow at the south.

TABLE 4
Comparative Missouri River Horse Prices

Snake $\longrightarrow$	Crow $\longrightarrow$	Mandan-Hidatsa village price
$1-2	$2-4	$6-8

good horse . . . and paid what I thought a good price for him."[28] He subsequently disclosed that the valuation of those goods would be doubled before they were traded west – making them worth two hundred MB.[29]

Lewis and Clark also experienced this process of doubling before sale. They discovered, when bargaining with the Snake Indians for horses, that "an elegant horse may be purchased of the natives for a few beads or other paltry trinkets which in the United States would not cost more than one or two dollars." These Snake were at the western end of the Mandan-Hidatsa trade system. They traded their horses at what J.C. Ewers called the "Shoshoni rendezvous."[30] This trade mart was attended by the Snake, Flathead, Nez Perce, Ute and Crow Indians. The successful military campaigns of the Blackfoot-Cree alliance and of the Missouri Indians had driven them from the plains, and by 1805 this allowed the Crow to make peace with the now non-aggressive Snake and to open a trade in horses with them.

According to Ewers, the Crow, when they arrived at the Mandan-Hidatsa villages with these horses, demanded a "mark up of 100 per cent."[31] Using the price that Lewis and Clark paid the Snake as an approximate base price for the Shoshone rendezvous, this Crow demand would mean a price of between two and four dollars for each horse sold to the Mandan-Hidatsa. The resale price that the villagers affixed to horses from the Crow would have been between six and eight dollars each, depending on the qualify of the animal.

The evidence of Lewis and Clark and the results of Ewers's research is summarized in Table 4, which shows the cost of one horse as it moved eastward through the trade system. *doubling*

When Henry purchased one horse at the villages for a hundred MB, he paid the following basket of European goods: "1 new gun, 400 Balls and powder, 1 Chiefs scarlet Coat, 1 copper kettle, 1 hand axe, 1 iron lance, 1 broad bead belt, 2 wampum hair pipes, 2 wampum shell pipes, 1/2 lb. Blue beads, 1 doz. brass rings, 1 doz. hawk bells, 1/2 doz. flints, 1/2 doz. worms, 1/2 doz. awls, 2 large knives, 1 small saw, 1 hornful White powder."[32] Applying the same doubling system outlined above and keeping the goods at the Red River valuation, this basket, traded from east to west through the system, produced interesting results relative to the price of one horse and the number of horses obtainable for the total value of the basket (see Table 5).

If the Mandan could buy one horse for fifty MB, then by an upward adjustment

TABLE 5
Comparison of Purchasing Power along the Missouri River

	Snake ←	Crow ←	Mandan-Hidatsa ←	Red River
price of 1 horse	25 MB	50 MB	100 MB	
number of horses	4=100 MB	2=100 MB	1=100 MB	

of the value of the basket to two hundred MB they could purchase four times as many horses with the same goods as could the Cree. Even if the Cree revalued the basket upward, the revaluation could only have caused a similar revaluation in the villages and could not have affected the ratio of purchasing power that had been set up by the west-to-east system of doubling.

It is difficult to believe that this situation could have existed when the Cree-Assiniboine were the exclusive source of European goods. The disadvantageous position of the Cree-Assiniboine was most likely caused by their adoption of a plains way of life, the consequent reduction in beaver trapping, and the effects of the arrival of white traders. The traders' presence in the village may have also caused a rise in the price of horses in an effort by the Mandan-Hidatsa to increase their supply of European goods through means other than beaver hunting.[33] As early as 1795 the Canadian traders were supplied with horses from the villages.[34] In 1806 Henry paid a hundred MB for a horse, while James Sutherland reported paying only forty-five MB in 1796.[35] It is even possible that the Mandan-Hidatsa became selective about the type of European goods to be traded for horses. In 1804 one HBC trader travelled to the villages with "tobacco, beads, and other merchandise to trade for furs, and a few guns to be traded for horses."[36]

The price increase is an indication of a much more serious adjustment in the trade system. Fur-trade prices were based on the white traders' consideration of overhead, including inventory, transportation, salaries and expected profits in European or Canadian markets. Prior to 1821, the year of the amalgamation of the rival companies, these prices were also determined in part by the state of competition. The Cree and Assiniboine acquired their European goods from these white traders at rates determined in that manner. There was nothing crippling in this situation while the Cree and Assiniboine were the exclusive suppliers to the village. But when the Mandan-Hidatsa made direct contact with the white traders, the Cree-Assiniboine were caught between two pricing systems. The ability of the Cree and Assiniboine to acquire European goods (which they could turn to the purchase of horses) remained tied to the European price structure. The pricing of horses, of course, was determined by the Mandan-Hidatsa and not by the white traders. The one-hundred-percent increase in horse prices (forty-five MB to a hundred MB) was not matched by a commensurate increase in the price of beaver. The market price of beaver between 1784 and 1805 rose only fifty percent.[37] To remain competitive in the villages the Cree and Assiniboine had to adhere to the prices for European goods determined by white traders. The result was that as horse prices rose and the number of beaver skins traded declined, the Cree and Assiniboine found it difficult to maintain adequate purchasing power in the Mandan-Hidatsa system.[38]

In response to this situation, the Cree-Assiniboine developed two courses of action. Both were implemented between 1795 and 1806 and neither of them brought satisfactory long-term results. John McKay, the HBC trader at Brandon House in 1805, recorded in his journal that "the Mandane and Big Bellies [Hidatsa] has 132 new Guns, all from Red River, no wonder these Indians is always in want of that article, as fast as they take them in Debt they give them away to the Mandals or Big Bellies they get nothing in return but Indian Corn and Buffalo Robes this is a great means why they often slip their Debts."[39]

Trading corn and buffalo robes for guns was a short-sighted arrangement. Corn was used even now, throughout the period to 1870, by the Plains Cree–Assiniboine as a supplement to their diet and as a safeguard against seasons when they could find no buffalo. In 1804 two hundred lodges of Assiniboine "passed the winter at the Forks of the Little Mississouri [and] sent daily to the village to barter for corn."[40] A good part of the corn purchased was consumed rather than used in trade. Buffalo robes, too, although they could be traded to the British and Canadian traders, brought small returns.

Of course, John McKay's suggestion that the Cree-Assiniboine got nothing for their guns but corn and buffalo robes is not quite accurate. They traded for horses as well. In 1806 Henry, for example, noted that Old Crane and his band, on their way home from the villages, were "all provided with horses and loaded with corn." But the resale value of these horses once they were in the hands of the Cree and the Assiniboine plummeted downward. As early as 1795 traders on the Red and Assiniboine rivers remarked that horses purchased in the Mandan villages were "very expensive." Only in 1818 was some more specific indication given of that price relative to horse prices on the southeastern plains. Peter Fidler noted that "horses traded there [the villages] were very dear, near double the prices we give for them in this Quarter."[41] This margin of difference probably fluctuated between 1795 and 1817 so that the Cree-Assiniboine loss during some years may have been less than fifty percent, but it would still seem to have been a loss. Horses, then, along with corn and buffalo robes, were not highly profitable items for them in their dealings with white traders.

According to McKay's outline of the process, the Cree and Assiniboine, having taken guns for the Mandan-Hidatsa trade on credit and being unable to make up their debt through the sale of items subsequently purchased at the village, would "often slip their debts." This technique short-circuited both the native and European trade systems. They in effect acquired European articles at no cost except their reputation, and turned a profit irrespective of the rate of exchange charged by the Mandan-Hidatsa. During this period of competition between the fur companies, they could for a while escape retribution. Their behaviour, though, was that of thieves, and the white traders would not allow themselves to be plundered for long. A short journal entry by John Linklater, a British trader, outlined the fate of an Indian who employed this technique: "I got a horse for my Debt from a Cree as I could get no other mode of payment."[42] The profit of stealing was taken from him.

By choosing the second course of action the Cree and Assiniboine were trying to turn back the clock to the period when their role as the sole suppliers of European goods to the villages had given them considerable leverage. On two occasions, the first in 1804 and the second in 1806, they decided to block "any Communication, between their traders & the Missouri Indians, as they wish to Engross that trade themselves."[43] Between 1804 and 1806, the traders were forced to carry their guns fully charged. Alexander Henry said, if they were caught on the track to the villages, the Cree and Assiniboine "would certainly deprive us of our horses . . . and even pillage us of our property and perhaps murder us all, as they disapprove of our taking Arms and Ammunition to the Missouri."[44] This move was directed toward regaining their position as the sole source of European goods for the villages and the benefits of that position. It was doomed to failure by the very contradictions inherent in its conception. The white traders were expected to allow themselves to be cut off from the Mandan-Hidatsa and at the same time to carry on a peaceful trade with their would-be oppressors.

The Cree-Assiniboine strategies of non-payment of debt and blockade bear the mark of frustration. Their favoured position in a system they helped to build and defend in the eighteenth century had disappeared. The twin pressures of the Mandan-Hidatsa system of price doubling and the stable fur-pricing system reshaped the Cree-Assiniboine role from one of partnership with the Mandan-Hidatsa to that of client. They were unable to discover a workable policy that would redress the system of pricing in their favour. They could remain within the native trade system only on the terms set by the Mandan-Hidatsa. They were still a supplementary source of European goods, however, and remained a useful ally against the Sioux.

The Cree and Assiniboine, however, were impatient with their lot. The high price for horses prevented them from purchasing as many as they needed. As late as 1804 Alexander Henry met a war party of three hundred Cree and Assiniboine warriors, only half of whom were mounted, the remainder being forced to walk and to fight on foot.[45] This situation caused internal pressure, some of which was channelled into the Cree–Gros Ventre disputes in the northern and western plains, but a residue of which made itself felt in this southeastern area. In 1796 "a number of Crees and Assinipoils, set out for the Mandals to steal horses."[46]

The periods of instability apparent in Cree-Assiniboine–Mandan-Hidatsa relations between 1794 and 1805 were based on the attempts by the Cree and Assiniboine to rebuild a profitable position for themselves in the trade system, and on the shocks of horse thefts by Cree and Assiniboine warriors. By 1806 these thefts had become so common, by the Assiniboine at least, that the villagers' "invariable rule now [was] to put the horses every night in the same lodge with the family."[47] This trend toward stealing Mandan-Hidatsa horses was the beginning of the end for the trade and military alliance between the Cree-Assiniboine and the Mandan-Hidatsa.

— as a result, Cree-Assiniboine increasingly stole from M-H horses; thining of alliance.

The Breakdown of
Cree-Assiniboine – Mandan-Hidatsa
Relations, 1806 to 1837

6

The Cree and Assiniboine raiders who had begun to prey upon the horse herds of
the Mandan-Hidatsa were attacking a force which had changed significantly since
the 1730s. By the early 1800s the Mandan-Hidatsa had developed considerable
military capability. The villages themselves were the core of their strength. David
Thompson discovered a design underlying the jumble of lodges that composed a
village. Sitting on a buffalo robe in one of these lodges, he drew on the sandy floor
the plan of an English town. His hosts studied it in silence, then, shaking their heads,
they stated, "In these straight streets we see no advantage the inhabitants have over
their enemies."[1] Thompson was forced to concede that "their manner of building
and disposition of the houses, is probably the best, for they build for security, not
for convenience."[2]

Because of the solid village base, the Mandan-Hidatsa had a strong defensive
position; they were able to maintain a constant reserve of provisions in the event
that an attacking force confined them to their village, cutting them off from the buffalo herds.[3] They also took measures to guarantee adequate fire power. "Arms and
Ammunition . . . are very essential articles for their defense, and accordingly every
individual has a stock of Ball and Powder laid up in case of any sudden emergencies."[4]

Two factors were involved in giving the Mandan-Hidatsa confidence to become
an effective offensive power: one was their involvement in buffalo hunting, an activity which necessarily brought discipline and coordination to a mounted force;
the other was the flow of guns from the Northeast. They even organized campaigns
against the Sioux.[5] Furthermore, peace with the Crow and Cheyenne released them
from reliance on the Cree-Assiniboine as the sole source of military aid.[6]

Against the background of this military strength the Mandan council was convened on 17 November 1804 to consider relations with the Cree and Assiniboine and to determine their policy toward these now troublesome people.[7] Their deliberations were long and involved, and it was not until the following day that Black Cat, one of the leading participants, informed Lewis and Clark, who were making preparations to winter in the village, of the result of the meeting. "The council decided that they would not resent the recent insults from the Assiniboine and Knistinaux, until they had seen whether we had deceived them or not in our promises of furnishing them with arms and ammunition."[8] In answer to this, Lewis and Clark advised them "to continue at peace that supplies of every kind would no doubt arrive for them, but that time was necessary to organize the trade."[9] The overriding consideration in the council had obviously been the imperative to keep open the lines of supply. Cree and Assiniboine transgressions would have to be ignored until the promises of the white explorers were fully realized. Only with the acquisition of a reliable alternate source of European goods could the Mandan afford to end their association with the Cree and Assiniboine.

The Lewis and Clark promise was based on the assumption that their flag of exploration would be quickly followed by the flag of trade. They were correct. In 1807 Manuel Lisa, co-founder of the Missouri Fur Company, made contact with the Mandan and built Lisa's Fort at the junction of the Big Knife and Missouri rivers. This post was maintained until 1812. Other traders such as Ramsay Crooks, later president of the American Fur Company, and his partner, Robert McClellan, worked this area of the Missouri between 1807 and 1817.[10]

These early years of the American trade on the Missouri were not without serious problems, however. John Bradbury, an American travelling up the Missouri in 1809, said, "[the Sioux] had been waiting for us eleven days with a decided intention of opposing our progress."[11] In the subsequent council, the Sioux chief recited a litany of excuses for a blockade, claiming that "they were at war with the Ricaras, Mandans and Minaterees [Hidatsa] and that it would be an injury to them if these nations were furnished with arms and ammunition."[12] Two years later W. Brakenbridge, an American travelling in Lisa's company, had the same experience.[13]

These blockades, meeting with uneven success, continued over the next ten years. By the 1820s the Arikara had begun to employ them. Then, in 1823 they made a fatal mistake: they killed thirteen traders attached to W.H. Ashley's fur brigade. After two campaigns of retaliation, the first led by General H. Leavenworth and the second by Colonel H. Atkinson, the Arikara were pacified and the Missouri was opened for safe passage.[14] The construction of western posts then proceeded unopposed. The history of the North Saskatchewan two decades earlier now became the experience of the Missouri. James Kipp built a post for the Columbia Fur Company adjacent to the villages in 1823. In 1828 the American Fur Company bypassed the villages, constructing Fort Union at the junction of the Yellowstone and Missouri rivers. Three years later that company built Fort Clark, the most famous of the Mandan-Hidatsa posts.[15] The monopoly exercised by Indian middlemen disappeared.

These military events and the establishment of a secure flow of goods from the Southeast were bound to cause a realignment of plains military patterns. But in 1804 the existing pattern, insofar as the Cree, Mandan-Hidatsa and Assiniboine were concerned, was based on a flow of European goods from the Northeast. There is little doubt that as the Mandan-Hidatsa gained confidence in this southeastern route, and as Cree-Assiniboine depredations continued, the Mandan-Hidatsa were freed from their reluctance to strike back against the horse thieves.

Even though Cree-Assiniboine–Mandan-Hidatsa relations were increasingly fragile, the Cree and Assiniboine continued to undertake massive campaigns against the common enemy, the Sioux. In 1806, after a series of small and inconclusive engagements, fourteen hundred Cree, Assiniboine and Ojibwa warriors congregated at the Turtle Mountains. This large party began its journey but was plagued by dissension because the warriors "were assembled from a vast extent of country of dissimilar feelings and dialects and of the whole fourteen hundred, not one would acknowledge any authority superior to his own will. It is true that ordinarily they yield a certain degree of obedience to the chief . . . but the obedience . . . continues no longer than the will of the chief corresponds entirely with the inclination of those he leads." Individually and in groups, warriors dropped out. Murders and horse stealing caused further division until they were within two days' march of the Sioux villages when "four hundred were all that remained,"[16] so they turned and went home.

The year 1806 began poorly for the Mandan. They lost men in two military campaigns and young people as well "to the hooping cough which was then raging throughout the country."[17] In July their situation improved markedly. The Sioux and Cheyenne arrived at the Mandan-Hidatsa villages and peace was made. While the four tribes were camped together a great commotion broke out.

After waiting in suspense for some time, we [Alexander Henry] were informed that the uproar proceeded from the arrival of Twelve Asineboines [led by Old Crane] a party of these people having arrived at the Village just after we had left it, now taking the advantage of the Big Bellies [Hidatsa] and Mandans, being more numerous than the Schines and Sioux had followed our tracks to the camp. The Schines upon being informed of their coming were fully determined to kill them as those people are most inveterate enemies to each other. But as they came upon our road and in a manner under the protection of our party the latter [Mandan and Hidatsa] were resolved instantly to defend and protect them.[18]

The decision by the Mandan in 1804, based on the need to maintain the northeast connection, seems to have remained operative to this point. The arrival of Old Crane's party caused the peace to become somewhat unsettled, although no actual fighting took place.

It is possible that this Sioux-Hidatsa-Mandan accord had been initiated by the latter, for during the summer they and the Hidatsa went to war against the Arikara. The peace could have been nothing more than a ploy to isolate that nation. Exactly how long this pattern lasted is not known. In 1809 the Sioux chief who spoke to John Bradbury named the Mandan as one of his enemies and, subsequent to that council, Bradbury met a Mandan-Hidatsa-Arikara war party bound for Sioux territory.[19]

Little evidence exists concerning the state of military affairs on the southeastern plains between 1807 and 1817. It is known that the Sioux kept up their attempts to blockade the Missouri. In the summer of 1809, Alexander Henry discovered that a powerful force of Assiniboines "had assembled upon the banks of the Missouri to go to War [and] when all their Firearms were collected and counted the total was 1,100 Guns." These warriors may well have been headed for the Hidatsa villages, for in the following year, "within Cry of the [Brandon] House,"[20] the Assiniboine were caught unprepared by a party of Hidatsa. Luckily, they escaped without one casualty.

Records contain no mention of Cree military activity throughout this period and up to 1817. It is probable that they maintained their yearly forays against the Sioux. By 1817, however, a state of war existed between them and the Mandan. In that year the Cree, upon sighting a band of sixty Mandan warriors, disbanded a buffalo hunt and fled to the safety of Brandon House.[21] Between 1817 and 1821 the Cree, for the first time in their plains history, began to take military and political action independent of, and at times opposed to, the positions adopted by their Assiniboine allies.

On 9 November 1817 a jubilant Assiniboine war party returned to Brandon House after a raid on the Mandan. They proclaimed that they were "going there again to War in about a Month & to steal horses."[22] But the Cree under the leadership of "The Little Sonneau . . . speak of going there soon on purpose to renew Terms of Friendship between both tribes which has long existed between them."[23] On 15 December Peter Fidler, who was then the master of Brandon House, wrote: "A few days before Our People reached their villages an Embassy of Sioux had departed for their own lands they had been to renew their former alliance and our party understood that both tribes have agreed to make war in Company in the spring against the Stone Indians who trade in the Assiniboine River."[24] The Assiniboine displayed a typical reaction; they attempted to blockade the track to the Missouri.[25]

Even in the face of this Mandan-Hidatsa-Sioux alliance and the Assiniboine blockade, the Cree persisted in pursuing their policy of peace. On 27 January 1818 the Cree told Fidler that they "are all going to visit the Mandanes in a friendly manner very soon."[26] They passed part of that winter in the Mandan villages and negotiated an amicable settlement. It is hard to believe that they did not discuss the Sioux-Mandan plans for the spring. In March they returned to Brandon House accompanied by a Mandan brave.[27] The next two months passed quietly. Then, on 1 May twelve Mandan warriors appeared at the Canadian post on the Qu'Appelle River and announced that "a great body of them is coming to war when the new Grass is about 2 Inches long."[28] As this news spread among the camps, the Assiniboine retreated to the north side of the Assiniboine River.[29] The Cree remained unperturbed. If the threatened war party did come, the Assiniboine managed to avoid it, for no battle has been recorded.

During the summer of 1818 three Assiniboine warriors fell in with Little Sonneau's band and treacherously murdered the Mandan, who had returned to live with the Cree after the Mandan peace settlement. This action may have been deliberately designed to disrupt the Mandan-Hidatsa-Cree peace and to force the Cree into active support of the Assiniboine against marauding Sioux-Mandan-Hidatsa war parties. The Cree, however, took the risk of travelling to the villages, unprepared for war, to return the dead men's hair and "to trade horses."[30] Therein lay the basis of Cree determination. They seem to have realized that the Assiniboine policy only cut them off from the horse mart and brought about the powerful combination of Sioux and Mandan-Hidatsa forces that could easily lead to successful incursions into their territory.

Cree determination was matched by astute Mandan-Hidatsa diplomacy. In their alliance with the Cree on one hand and the Sioux on the other, they were successfully juggling two opposites. Their alliance with the Sioux added to the security of the Missouri as the southeastern source of goods and their accord with the Cree assured access to the British and Canadians and visits from Cree traders. Even if the Sioux attacked the Cree, as they did in the spring of 1819,[31] the Mandan had managed to neutralize the Cree and isolate the Assiniboine. With Sioux aid they could deal severely with the Assiniboine.

In 1819 the Assiniboine seem to have recovered from the shock of the Sioux-Mandan-Hidatsa alliance and their abandonment by the Cree. On 4 June "60 Tents of Stone Indians, are going to war against the Mandans."[32] Two months later twenty more Assiniboine warriors set out for the villages and the Cree organized a raid against the Sioux in retaliation for their spring defeat. Neither their campaign against the Sioux nor the Assiniboine attacks on the Mandan prevented the Cree from once again going to trade in the villages.[33] By 1820 it began to look as if this new military and trade pattern, which excluded the Assiniboine, was becoming settled. Yet, within three years it had disintegrated.

The common Cree-Assiniboine antipathy to the Sioux nation undoubtedly saved the Cree-Assiniboine alliance which, since 1817, seemed to have been drifting toward a violent rupture. By this period the Sioux had expanded into the area between the Mississippi and the Missouri.[34] To the north was the territory of their historic enemies, the Cree, Assiniboine and Ojibwa. If the Cree wished to keep open their trade with the Mandan-Hidatsa they would have to contend with the continued threat of the Sioux. Although the Assiniboine were no longer an asset in Cree relations with the Mandan-Hidatsa, Assiniboine military aid had been valuable in Cree hostilities with the Sioux. The price of Assiniboine aid would logically have been Cree compliance with the Assiniboine position on the Mandan.

In the early 1820s the pace of warfare quickened and the Cree and Assiniboine moved closer together until their alliance was reborn in its old form. In 1820 the Cree participated in the first recorded campaign with the Assiniboine since before 1817.[35] That winter "4 or 5 Indians [no tribe given] in the vicinity of Red River had been killed by the Mandans,"[36] causing another war party to assemble at Portage la Prairie in the spring of 1821. The Mandan struck again in the winter of 1822 but were repulsed by the Assiniboine.[37] This may have been the decisive blow. In the afternoon of 8 March 1823, "two Crees arrive [at Fort Ellice]. . . . One of them called the Eagle. They inform us that all the Crees are assembling . . . to go to war. The Mandales have already made their appearance at the Mountain and killed one Stone Indian."[38]

This one campaign not only completely snapped the Mandan-Cree peace; it also finally totally broke the Cree-Assiniboine–Mandan-Hidatsa alliance, after years of questionable solidarity. Events of the next decade bore this out. James Kipp of the Columbia Fur Company built a post adjacent to the villages and in that same year the Federal troops of the Leavenworth and Atkinson campaigns attacked the Arikara. Nothing demonstrates more clearly the end of this old alliance, and the Mandan-Hidatsa abandonment of the northeastern trade route, than Mandan actions in 1831 and 1832. On 25 September 1831 they attacked and killed two HBC freemen within a mile of Brandon House. A month later they reappeared, ambushed a work party and drove them back into the security of the post. The following autumn a group of Company employees was attacked by a party of Mandan.[39]

On their part, the Cree and Assiniboine continued joint horse-stealing excursions and war parties. They were then completely cut off from every source of horses. Then, in the spring of 1831, La Quatre, the principal Cree chief in the Assiniboine River area, told the master of Fort Pelly that during the previous winter a "Crow Indian Chief has Sent pressing Messages to them to come and meet them

- Cree - Assiniboine alliance renewed against the Sioux (1820); break down of alliances w/the villages.

at a certain place holding out all offers of friendship that he would conduct them back out of all danger with a strong party of his young men and would also supply them with Horses at very Moderate prices." The Cree seemed completely surprised by this development. Their hunts were abandoned and the winter was spent in councils. As in their peace with the Mandan in 1817, the Cree were once again drawn by the possibility of establishing direct contact with a supply of horses. Yet, there was some hesitancy, some suspicion of Crow motives. The HBC was sure that the invitation was an attempt by American traders to obtain control of Cree hunts. The Cree doubted this but they did intend to visit those traders "with a view of learning how the Indians are treated by the Americans."[40]

On 10 June 1831 the Cree, with some Saulteaux, left the Fort Pelly area to visit the Crow. The question of Crow motivation had still not been settled and, as they travelled, their doubts may have grown. The Crow invitation could have been intended as bait to draw them into a Crow or even a Mandan-Hidatsa trap, and when they least expected it they would be ambushed by their would-be trading partners. Such fears were well-founded, for later, on the banks of the Missouri, they were indeed attacked by the Mandan. The fighting was desperate, and finally the Mandan were forced to abandon "their Horses, Guns and even their dress and only escaped by their dexterity in Swimming across the Missouri River."[41]

This defeat was only one of the disasters which befell the Mandan in the 1830s. By 1833 the Mandan could count among the ranks of their enemies the Blackfoot, Assiniboine, Sioux, Pawnee, Arikara, Cheyenne, Cree and Arapaho.[42] Only the Hidatsa and Crow remained faithful to them. The Crow, who were reputed to have a stock of between nine and ten thousand horses, continued to trade their animals to them and to exchange visits with their Hidatsa relatives.[43] But now the Mandan had no one with whom to trade these horses. The western extension of American posts beyond the Mandan villages had released the plains tribes from Mandan influence and must be seen as one of the causes of the military pattern just noted.

Although conditions seemed ripe for a new Cree-Assiniboine-Mandan-Hidatsa alliance, it did not come about, and there is no evidence showing that overtures were made in that direction by either side. The Cree and Assiniboine, although judged poor in horses, maintained their military pressure on the villages. According to Maximilian, Prince of Wied, they were "very daring and often approach the villages . . . either singly or in small parties, and sometimes surprise individuals and shoot them."[44] American trader Francis A. Chardon witnessed the departure of three hundred Cree and Assiniboine warriors bound for the Mandan-Hidatsa villages.[45] Two years later he witnessed the death of the Mandan nation.

In 1837 smallpox spread throughout the Mandan villages. By August only twenty-three warriors were left alive.[46] The Mandan tried to recruit their strength

— 1830s → Mandan-Hidatsa horse trading syst. is weakened as war enemies surround them 1837 → smallpox epidemics; no alliance w/ Cree-Ass.

by inviting the Arikara, who had been moving up the Missouri in the face of Sioux pressure, to join them in the nearly empty villages. This arrangement proved unworkable and in June 1838 "the few remaining Mandans that were living with the Rees all started up to remain with the Minnetaree [Hidatsa], as they cannot agree with the Rees, as the latter are continually stealing their women."[47] So after years of settled and prosperous occupation of these villages, the remaining Mandan were exiles once again. The abandoned villages did not long outlive their builders. Before daylight on Wednesday 7 January 1839, Chardon, standing on the wall of Fort Clark, "beheld the Mandan Village all in flames. The lodges being all made of dry Wood, and all on fire at the same time, Made a splendid sight, the Night being dark – this Must be an end to What was once called the Mandan Village."[48]

THE HORSE WARS, 1810 TO 1850

III

Overleaf: Combat between Blackfoot, Assiniboine and Cree Indians, Fort McKenzie, Montana, 28 August 1833; sketch from *Illustrations to Maximilian, Prince of Wied's Travels in the Interior of North America* , plate no. 75 (Glenbow Archives, Calgary, NA-2347-1)

Some Aspects of Plains Cree Social and Political Organization

7

[margin note: break down of old alliances] *[margin note: buffalo wars]*

The years from 1810 to 1850 constitute a distinct era in the history of the Plains Cree: it is a long, middle period which existed between two eras of significant change. By 1810 the Cree's commanding, middleman role in the European fur trade had been circumscribed, and their native trade systems had been undermined by the extension of the sources of European goods into the home territory of every tribe on the Canadian plains. Familiar military patterns, including the Blackfoot--Cree alliance, had broken down, and Cree-Mandan-Hidatsa relations had entered their final phase. By this time the Cree had completed their transition to a plains way of life, although they continued to receive woodland recruits all through this and the next era. This cultural metamorphosis lent a new emphasis to the importance of the horse trade, which in turn contributed to the failure of Cree alliances with both the Blackfoot and Mandan-Hidatsa. *[margin note: - break down of alliances, disappearance of middleman position - complete transition to plains life way]*

The middle period ended about 1850. The subsequent era, 1850 to 1870, was a time of crisis. The buffalo herds, the very basis of plains subsistence, began a rapid decline, which brought a new focus to plains warfare and highlighted a new trend in Cree economic behaviour. It also, most significantly, induced the intensification of Cree awareness of territory, their nation, their relationship with the Europeans and the effects of the fur trade. *[margin note: - decline of buffalo herds]*

What then is the nature of the 1810--1850 era? Certainly, the Cree continued their conscious and rational attempts to construct new military and trade patterns to replace those which had failed. The end of territorial wars and wars waged to protect favoured fur-trade positions did not eliminate the substantive motives for military patterns. War remained a communal undertaking designed to serve Cree self-interest. However, this period also encompasses the development by the Cree of their version of plains society. Thus it contains all the romance, the colour and *[margin note: development of a separate and definite social organization]* the particular cultural traits which are the hallmarks of the popular depiction of the plains Indians and their society. Attention should be given to the size, structure and motive forces of that society, and the influence of certain cultural traits, not only because of their inherent interest but also because it is clear that there was a vital connection between the external world of war and trade, and the internal structure and function of band institutions. The external and internal world fit together in intimate interdependence. The drive to achieve a defined group self-interest by constructing and manipulating external relations was motivated by, and contributed to, the system of relationships among individual males. These relationships in turn were a determinant of social and political organization, and also contributed to the stability and prosperity of the group. Because of the interplay between the world within the band circle and the world outside of it, an outline of various aspects of Cree social and political organization forms an important prologue to a discussion of the military and trade chronology of this period and of the subsequent one as well.

CREE POPULATION AND BAND BREAKDOWN, 1810 TO 1850

The size of the Indian population in any period prior to enumeration under the treaty system was not precisely recorded. This, of course, does not downgrade the utility or the importance of the approximate estimates that were recorded by early travellers and traders. The problem they faced in establishing a rough census was well expressed by Alexander Henry in his cautionary preface to an estimate of the Cree: "To find the exact number it would be a difficult task as they are dispersed over such a vast extent and frequently intermix with other nations."[1] It was not until the onset of the reserve period that the Plains Indians could be separated, made to stand still and be counted. Early accounts were hampered by this Indian mobility and the limited view of the enumerator. This in turn led to vagueness and wild variation in the estimates. H.R. Schoolcraft provides three estimates which illustrate this point: "1736 Cristineaux, Ounepegan Lake – 60; 1764 Christineaux, Ounepegan Lake – 3,000; 1812 Killisteneaux, Ounepegan Lake – 500."[2]

To this problem of Indian mobility must be added the indefinite effects of various epidemics, especially smallpox, on the demographic profile of the Plains Indians. The first of these calamities was noted by La Vérendrye in 1737 when "the Winnipeg Cree . . . at Fort Maurepas had all died of small-pox."[3] There is no doubt that "all" was intended to represent a substantial proportion, but a proportion of what total is not known.

The effect, both psychological and demographic, is much clearer for the second, and most infamous of the plagues. In the years between 1780 and 1782, as death swept down upon them, the Indians were stunned with incredulity; how could the pox move from person to person? "We had no belief that one man could give it to another, any more than a wounded man could give his wound to another." They abandoned their hunts, fled from their dying relations and friends and even threw away furs "to the good Spirit, that they might live." Nor was it uncommon for "the father of a family, whom the infection had not reached, to call them around him to represent the cruel sufferings and horrid fate of their relatives, from the influence of some evil spirit who was preparing to extirpate their race; and to incite them to baffle death, with all its horrors, by their own poniards." The landscape presented a desolate picture, "the Indians lying Dead about the Barren Ground like rotten sheep, their Tents left standing and Wild beasts Devouring them." The traders could only stand aside and watch. William Tomison reported his sincere distress to the Company's owners: "I do assure your Honours it cuts me to the Heart to see the Miserable condition they are in and not being able to help them."[4]

The passing of the plague left the Indians in a stupor. It was only with difficulty that many survivors could be coaxed back into the normal pattern of life.[5] Those who survived believed, according to many white witnesses, that "the Great Master of Life had delivered them over to the Evil Spirit for their wicked courses; and for many years afterward those who escaped the deadly contagion, strictly conformed themselves to their own code of moral laws."[6] From the estimates of the death toll it appears that the Evil Spirit had chastised them very severely. Edward Umfreville held that not more than one in fifty survived, and Alexander Henry believed that two-thirds of the Cree nation succumbed.[7]

The Cree were much more fortunate in the one epidemic that fell in the period between 1810 and 1850. By then the traders were no longer completely helpless, since they had some medical aid to offer. In 1837 smallpox returned. It first appeared on the Canadian plains among "a band of half crees half assiniboin called the young dogs as they speak both languages but neither correctly." William Todd, master of Fort Pelly, was forewarned of its approach from the Missouri and worked hard to vaccinate all the Cree of that area. He even taught the procedure to some Indians and reported that one man "vaccinated his own family and about 20 of his connexions." Although there are no post journal references to programs of vaccination in other areas of the plains, J. Rae, the arctic explorer, stated that "a gentleman at the Saskatchewan vaccinated all the Cree Indians that came in; and there was scarcely a single case occured among the tribe." In this manner the plague was confined to the Blackfoot and "principally the Assiniboine," and of course the Mandan who, having violently rejected the British traders, cut themselves off from this medical assistance.[8] The Cree seemed to have escaped with relatively few losses.

The evidence seems conclusive that the population of western Indians declined significantly in the years between 1780 and 1782, that estimates of Cree population after this plague would represent only a fraction of the early eighteenth-century population, and that the Cree population between 1810 and 1850 should not show a dramatic variation due to the plague of 1837.

Probably the most reliable early estimate of Indian population is found in William McGillivray's short 1809 work entitled *Sketch of the Fur Trade of Canada.*[9] His total count for the plains was 30,000 individuals. He subsequently broke this aggregate down by tribe, although his categories of enumeration are inconsistent. The estimates are provided either by number of tents, number of families or number of individuals. The logic of his figures discloses a constant relationship among the three categories: 1 tent = 1.4 families = 14 individuals. Using these ratios, one could convert his figures and recast his census (see Table 6).

Alexander Henry's 1810 accounting concludes with a total of 28,000,[10] a figure remarkably close to McGillivray's aggregate figure. In 1857 Sir George Simpson, inland governor of the HBC, told the Select Committee of the British Parliament that the total plains population had declined to 25,000.[11] These totals taken together would indicate a net loss of at least three- to five thousand Indians during the period between 1810 and 1850. Although it is impossible to judge the reliability of these estimates, they show an expected downward trend due to smallpox, venereal disease, scarlet fever, measles, whooping cough and warfare.

McGillivray's 1809 figure of 4,900 for the Plains Cree population is given support by Henry, who estimates their number at 4,200.[12] One wonders whether thereafter the Cree population followed the general downward trend which was exhibited by the total plains population. David Mandelbaum chose the figure 12,500 as the Cree total for 1860,[13] clearly suggesting an upward movement and implying that the force of natural increase and in-migration from the woodlands was more than adequate to compensate for death through disease and warfare.

Estimates from 1829 through to 1850 would tend to lend credence to Mandelbaum's position. General P. Porter, secretary of war in the American government of 1829, reported that the Cree population was three thousand.[14] G. Catlin, the artist, noted in 1832, "I have said before that they [the Cree] are about 3,000 in number – by that I mean but a small part of that extensive tribe, who are in the habit of visiting American Fur Company Establishments."[15] Prince Maximilian's estimate of the whole Cree tribe in 1833 was 7,440,[16] 2,540 higher than McGillivray's. A War Department report of 1836 lists the Cree at three thousand.[17] Unfortunately, the next estimate does not appear until 1860. It placed Cree population at 11,500,[18] a figure only a thousand short of Mandelbaum's estimate. These figures indicate an overall increase of 5,600. Given the fact that the Cree almost totally escaped the epidemic of 1837, Mandelbaum's suggestion is credible. Black-

TABLE 6
William McGillivray's Population Estimate, 1809

Tribe	Figures as given	Conversion to families	Conversion to individuals
Ojibwa	---	24	336
Cree	250 T	350	4,900
Assiniboine	230 T	322	4,508
Sarcee	---	60	840
Blackfoot	700 T	1,000	19,600
Gros Ventre	200 T	280	3,920
Total			34,104

foot losses in 1837 alone account for the decrease in the total plains population of three- to five thousand.

This Plains Cree population was grouped into a number of bands which were, after the family, the basic social and political unit of the tribe. Diamond Jenness states that the historic Cree had twelve bands, each with its own chief.[19] David Mandelbaum, whose work still represents the most significant anthropological contribution to Plains Cree study, discovered, for the period between 1860 and 1880, eight bands divided into two geographical headings. Both these positions should be accepted as correct. Mandelbaum stated that Cree bands "were loose and shifting units,"[20] meaning that the Cree were free to move from one band to another. The band as an institution was stable, but membership, specific territory, leadership and the number of bands fluctuated. Warfare, disease, the fortune of a leader ("the prestige and power of the leading chief was also an important factor in the cohesiveness of a band"),[21] or ecological factors could all cause the band count to be altered. This fluidity means that given band counts could not be accurate over a long span of time.

According to Mandelbaum's informants, Cree bands were grouped under two regional headings: the Downstream People and the Upstream People. The Calling River People (Qu'Appelle Valley), the Rabbit Skin People (the area between the Assiniboine and Qu'Appelle rivers), and the Touchwood Hills People (the area between Touchwood Hills and Long Lake) were the bands of the Downstream People. The Upstream People included the bands of the River People (the area between the North Saskatchewan and Battle rivers), the Beaver Hills People (west of the River People extending south to the Battle River), the House People (in the Fort Carlton area) and the Parkland People (situated just east of the former band).[22]

It is obvious, then, that the terms *Upstream* and *Downstream* relate to a division of Cree people into northwestern plains and southeastern plains groupings. This pattern was initially set in the early trade period by the Upstream People's (Saskatchewan Cree's) use of the Saskatchewan–Hayes River route to the Bay posts and the Downstream People's use of the Assiniboine–Red River and Lake Winnipeg waterways. It was subsequently reinforced by involvement in the particular trade and military patterns dominating the area – the Blackfoot and the Mandan-Hidatsa systems. There is no evidence, though, showing that these regional divisions were sharp enough to cause the growth of two separate Cree nations on the plains. Participation of Downstream People in the military events of the northwestern plains was evident in 1789, 1793, 1795 and 1802, and increased after 1802.

Edwin Denig, whose fur-trade career was centred in the southeastern plains, furnished a partial Cree band count which lends support to the idea of a constant biregional division. What is of immediate interest is Denig's concept that the whole Cree nation was represented by the Downstream People. He fails to acknowledge the existence of the Upstream People; in fact, he goes so far as to state that they (the whole Cree nation) could not sustain their position near the numerous northern tribes but were compelled to place several hundred miles of uninhabited territory between themselves and other more war-like nations.[23] Denig's suggestion of a southeastern retreat does not bear the scrutiny of primary evidence which details a constant Plains Cree presence in the Northwest, but it does emphasize the permanency of the regional division.

The Cree of the southeastern plains were, according to Denig's notes, divided into the eight bands:[24]

1 Chocab, or band of Eyes Open, 100 lodges, residing in the Qu'Appelle area.
2 Pay si e kan, or Striped, 40 to 50 lodges, near the Tinder Mountain.
3 Pis cha haw a chis, or Magpies, 30 to 40 lodges, near the Tinder Mountain.
4 Kee as Koo sis, or Small Gulls, 30 to 40 families, near the Qu'Appelle River.
5 The Painted Lodge, He Who Shoots the Bear with Arrows, The Little Eagle, and The Standing Bear, four small bands named after their leaders, about 130 to 140 lodges.
6 Ma tai tai ki ok, or Plusiers des Aigles, 300 lodges, led by Le Sonnant, near the Woody Mountains.
7 Band of She mare Kaw or La Lance, 350 lodges, near the Cypress and Prickly Pear Mountains.
8 Several small portions of the nation led by Red Fox, Iron Child, Muskeg gan etcetera, to the west of the Wood Mountains.

Although it is unfortunate that more definite population figures cannot be found and that a full band outline is not available for the Cree in the period between 1810 and 1850, factors have emerged which are probably more important. First, if Mandelbaum's trend is accepted, the Plains Cree population was growing in the face of disease and warfare, while other plains nations were losing numbers. Second, a regional division in the Cree nation was founded by geography and early trade systems, and was nurtured by military patterns prior to 1810. Third, the band count was not constant nor was band membership stable.

The basic suppleness of this band system should be noted. The system of complete transferability of membership among the bands gave the Cree social structure the elasticity to absorb, among other shocks, the blows of war and disease. As well, internal social pressures were given vent when a disaffected member could easily join another band. Aspiring warriors could fulfill their leadership ambitions by forming a new band without having to disrupt the existing political structure.[25] Although there is no evidence of "democracy," the band members' freedom of movement enforced a code of acceptable behaviour on the leadership, and made leaders seek concensus as the basis for decision making. The quality of leadership was a prime determinant in the cohesiveness and longevity of a band.[26]

PRESTIGE, INVESTMENT AND WELFARE

As well as the nature of leadership, the social and political organization of the Cree band and tribe reflect the generative forces at work behind the military and trade patterns. Prestige, which accrued to those who exhibited military valour, wealth and liberality, was the most important determinant governing social and political status. These factors were intimately linked, and enforced customary behaviour upon Cree males, channelling their lives into prescribed patterns. By following those prescribed patterns, the men competed with their peers to acquire increases in status until the ultimate level – chief – was reached. Yet, the very aspect of competition, upon which status was built, ensured the operation of an effective system of social welfare, through the redistribution of wealth.

The path to the position of chief was clearly marked. The young male Cree, unless he was a chief's son, began his social life without status, for unlike other plains people the Plains Cree had no age-grade societies. Participation in a raiding party would probably be the first act giving status to a young Cree man. If he displayed bravery he might be given, after one raid as a chief's son or after a number of raids if his family were of no great consequence, the title, "worthy young man." The next step was to be invited to join the warrior society, of which there was but one in each band. This society was led by the warrior chief, who was chosen by the warriors with his authority "confined to those activities performed by the Warriors as a group." The society was charged with guarding the line of march when the band travelled, policing the buffalo hunt and controlling the warriors when they were engaged in a military campaign. The last and paramount step was from a member of the warrior society, or warrior chief, to chief. The chief's position was often hereditary, but if a chief's son was considered incompetent, "some man of high prestige was acknowledged as successor."[27]

A man's war record established his status and was responsible for a rise from one level to the next. Mandelbaum's informants assured him that a man "who had not distinguished himself on the warpath could not be chief." Even ranking among chiefs was determined by their war exploits. When a number of chiefs met in council the status accorded each "did not depend on the size of his following but hinged largely on his war record." This record was composed of the history of the individual's participation in military campaigns or raids in which each of his deeds was given a particular value on a predetermined scale. "The criterion in ranking war exploits was the degree of danger to which the man was exposed while accomplishing the feat. Thus a man who shot an enemy while he himself was under fire outranked one who had killed an enemy from ambush. Similarly one who had killed his man with a club had more to his credit than one who had picked off his opponent with a rifle."[28]

The killing of an old man with grey hair was one of the highest deeds, for during an attack the old men usually remained inside the teepees with the women and children; a warrior would therefore have to penetrate the cordon of people protecting them. Paul Kane revealed that this accomplishment had a specific social consequence. In the tent of Chief Broken Arm, he noted, "Amongst our visitors was the son-in-law of the Chief and, according to Indian custom he took his seat with his back towards his father and mother-in-law never addressing them but through the medium of a third party. This rule is never broken through until the son-in-law proves himself worthy of personally speaking to him by having killed an enemy with white hairs."[29]

The concept that the more danger the warrior exposed himself to, the higher would be his deed's merit, was carried through to its logical end: "The highest deed of all was to make peace with a hostile tribe. It required great courage to approach the enemy unarmed, for hostile peoples usually shot the Cree at sight." Broken Arm, Kane's host in 1847, was not only "among the foremost and most renowned of their warriors," but was also "a remarkable exception to the generality of Indians, they call him the 'peacemaker,' and twice within the last two or three years he pushed his way alone into the Blackfoot country, and walked into the enemy's camp unarmed, with the peace pipe in his hand, exhorting them to peace, and offering them the alternative of killing him."[30]

Throughout his life the warrior was given the opportunity to reinforce his status by recounting his war record. These occasions included, among others, the sun dance, the giveaway dance and the Dakota dance. If a man were foolish enough to falsify his deeds, "he could be challenged by anyone who had been on war parties with him." This fact, plus the helpfulness of corroboration, guaranteed accurate reporting. Fine-day, Mandelbaum's primary informant, relating the deed that won him the title of worthy young man, stressed that "two Worthy Young Men who had been on the trip had seen me do all these things and that's why I became one of them."[31]

Although an outstanding war record was a prerequisite for advancement, wealth and liberality were also important. Open-handedness was a consideration in ranking a chief among his peers. "A chief had to give freely of his possessions to needy tribesmen, and usually set the pace on the occasions for ceremonial gift giving." It was incumbent upon the chief to be an energetic hunter as well as an intrepid warrior. One chief, Teimmskos, derived most of his prestige from his ability as a poundmaker, the individual responsible for the construction of the buffalo trap — the corral or pound. "In winter, people from distant places would seek his encampment to enjoy the abundance of meat secured under his guidance." Ceremonial communal feasts were "commonly made by the chiefs." Because "gift giving was a socially accepted method of mollifying an aggrieved person," it even played a role in the arbitration of disputes.[32]

[margin note: wealth + hunting abilities.]

[margin note: gift giving — as a way to elevate position in warring structures.]

Liberality was an expected and important mark of the chief's behaviour. It was also a device for increasing social status in conjunction with the individual's war record. The elevation from worthy young man to the warrior society was often delayed by the fact that "membership in the society entailed considerable expense; Worthy Young Men did not usually become Warriors until they acquired a number of . . . material possessions." Appropriate social mechanisms also existed to reward gift giving with enhanced status. Some of these, including the giveaway dance or the sitting-up-until-morning ceremony, were elaborate occasions while others were informal. During the dog feast, for example, "a Warrior would occasionally demonstrate his disdain of material possessions by having a new robe passed around on which the others wiped their greasy hands."[33]

Clearly related to individual gift giving was the practice of social investment which not only brought status but also worked as part of a Cree social welfare system. The individual would, having acquired a quantity of goods, distribute them among his friends, relatives and "the aged chiefs, and most respectable men of the tribe." The recipient could in turn use these goods in gift giving to raise his own status. But when the original owner needed a large amount of food for a feast, or required additional wealth to purchase a medicine bundle or a public position, such as the pipestem carrier, he had only to call in his investment. If a man failed to ful-

[margin note: redistribution.]

[margin note: individuals would be helped when needed based on their previous givings.]

fill his obligation to aid the donor, "his relatives . . . teased and mocked him until he settled his debt."[34] In this manner wealth was distributed throughout the band, raising the level of each family's status and ownership of material possessions yet still guaranteeing benefit for the individual who had originally acquired it.

Allied to this was a well-developed system of social welfare which extended to all members of the band. A chief, it was assumed, would display concern for the material welfare of his followers. "At ceremonies chiefs were expected to contribute a larger share of the feast than the other tribesmen." After a hunt when the meat was brought back into the camp, "the chief's wife dropped the choice parts in front of the tipis of the poor." As a wealthy man, the chief attached to his household orphans or the sons of poor families. "They were treated as members of the family, provided with clothes and food and were able to use the chief's horses. From the chief they received informal training in hunting and warfare. These workers . . . were to be found in the tipis of most men of high rank." Some chiefs were especially adroit at providing for the band. E. Denig described Chocab, Eyes Open, as a "chief of note . . . not so much as a warrior but as a prudent financier. . . . His duty as a leader, therefore, is to look out for the welfare of his people, to see they amass property, live comfortably and hunt with order, also to go at their head when they visit the fort to trade and endeavor to secure their . . . advantage by making the best bargain he can for them."[35]

The chief did not bear the burden of his office alone. He was supported by his relations, who in turn benefited from his position. Band members also supported the prestige and the office of their chief. The chief's crier and the caller, usually older men who could no longer take part in campaigns, were the officials who announced the chief's decisions and his deeds, and called men to council. Although chosen by the chief, many gifts of food and fine clothing were given to the incumbents by the band's leading men so that they "might not endanger the dignity of his position by being poorly clad."[36]

The warrior society also employed old men past the age of active participation in the competitive status process. These men functioned as criers and servers of food in the lodge. The society was also involved in the welfare of the band's poor. Mandelbaum learned that "old people or widows who were in need would kill a dog and bring it to the society lodge. The warriors feasted on the dog meat and then gave the donor whatever was requested."[37]

Customs relating to property display the Cree mix of individualism and social support. Food that was collectively procured was collectively distributed. But food which was obtained by the individual need not have been. There was no division of tribal hunting territory, either on an individual or a band basis. However, property such as guns, horses, hides, tents and dogs was individually owned, although use was allowed to all members of the extended family.[38] The distinctions of wealth which existed were blurred to some extent by the investment and welfare practices that distributed property through the band.

The quest for individual status, through participation in military campaigns and by demonstrating liberality through gift giving and disdain of material possessions, clearly displayed the intense competitiveness of Cree social and political life, and made a mockery of concepts of the exclusive communality of Plains Indian, hence Cree, society. John McDougall, the well-known western missionary, set forth a general condemnation that not only indicates how little he appreciated the real nature of Indian customs, but also illustrates the difficulties that many observers experienced in preventing their European values from colouring their analyses of Indian life. He wrote: "Tribal communism has always been hurtful to individuality, and without this no race of men can progress."[39] His use of the term *progress,* and the implication that its definition was simulation of white social and technological development, is enough to betray the bias of his position. His basic assumption, that is, that individualism and tribal communism (a term he does not define) could not reach full flower in the same pot, is not only logically suspect, but it is also incorrect in light of the evidence presented on individual efforts to acquire higher social ranking, the type of incipient class division that that implied, and the co-existence of a Cree social welfare system, which would seem to have constituted the real extent of Cree tribal communism. Since welfare was both an individual and a societal concern, tribal communalism should be seen as a function of the individual status quest, as well as a trait displaying not unexpected feelings of compassion and social conscience for the aged and less fortunate. Even the oldest enduring Canadian plains society, the Blackfoot, is portrayed by Oscar Lewis as individualistic and progressively materialistic.[40] Although there is no evidence that the Cree changed their prime focus from war to the acquisition of property, it has been demonstrated that individual action and initiative were the requirements for progression through the various levels of social rank.

It should not be assumed, however, that individual freedom was boundless. The rule of law (or the rule of custom) is everywhere evident in the structure of coup ranking, in the standardized conduct expected from members of the warrior society and even in the Cree religious system, where the Kieche Manito and Metchee Manito denoted a division between good and evil. On a more practical level, the sole decision-making authority of the chief and policing powers of the warrior society displayed executive authority and organized implementation of political decisions. And the practice of mocking and teasing of debtors is an example of the social pressures brought to bear on individuals to conform to social customs.

Although the band was the stage upon which the competition for status was

[margin notes: communal principals sustained by individual interests; social pressure, social control & rule of costum.]

[handwritten margin note: endeavours that brought prestige & p...]

enacted, it was outside the band and tribal setting that the individual acquired the *[handwritten: pos...]* raw material of prestige, that is, material goods and military honours. Bravery could be displayed only in warfare, either in organized campaigns or in raiding parties. Material goods could be acquired through trade, hunting and military adventure. It is obvious that the system could not function without trade and war. Band and tribal relations of the Cree with other tribes then bore directly upon internal social needs. External relations in the period before 1810 involved their participation in consciously constituted trade patterns and supportive military alliances and relationships. These patterns and alliances were, therefore, a rational approach to the problem of the acquisition of property that could be converted into status. In this respect the traders to the Blackfoot and to the Mandan-Hidatsa villages, and the participants in raids and organized campaigns against the Gros Ventre, Snake and Sioux tribes were in essence agents of a single societal demand working within an external tribal system, which induced the inflow of convertible material. *[handwritten: into status]*

[handwritten margin note: trade & military patterns.]

There is indeed evidence that this particular social purpose of war, which was a constant feature of Plains Cree warfare through to 1870, existed for the Saskatchewan Cree from the pre-plains period. The Saukamappee tradition indicates that individual ambition linked to status operated within the band decision to aid the Blackfoot against the Snake. Saukamappee informed Thompson that he would not have taken part in the second Blackfoot-Cree-Snake battle had it not been that his "wife's relations frequently intimated, that her father's medicine bag would be honoured by the scalp of a Snake Indian." That they were so rewarded is revealed when the war chief told the Cree and Assiniboine warriors "that if anyone had the right to the scalp of an enemy as a war trophy it ought to be us, who with our guns had gained the victory."[41]

[handwritten margin note: horses in trade, affect war patterns]

In the subsequent period, 1810 to 1850, the acquisition of horses, rather than of guns and other European technology, was the central factor in Plains Cree political life and was the object of carefully crafted trade patterns. Mandelbaum, viewing all material objects utilized by the Cree, designated the horse as "the standard of prestige value by means of which the status criteria of wealth, valor and liberality could be realized."[42] There is no doubt that the desire to acquire horses became a primary focus of the small raiding party which was designed specifically to function as an individual status quest mechanism. Fine-day's war record is simply a listing of successive status raids in which in each case horse stealing and brave deeds were the main components and an increase in status was the main derivative. Throughout the period between 1810 and 1850 there is abundant primary evidence that the launching of small war parties was a regular event in the Cree year.

Oscar Lewis has argued with respect to the Blackfoot that the horse and gun, and the resultant emergence of these small, mounted and deadly war parties, meant,

[handwritten: based on external, intertribal relations.]

in the 1810–1850 period, the decline of band, inter-band and tribal military under-takings, and that "raiding parties became essentially a means of personal aggran-disement in which tribal interests gave way to those of the individual."[43] This meant the disappearance of large organized campaigns directed toward tribal trade or military goals and, by implication, the disappearance of the type of trade patterns in existence prior to 1810 which relied upon coordinated group action. An almost senseless situation would have persisted in which, as Diamond Jenness wrote, "War and confusion reigned everywhere while the buffalo diminished apace."[44]

This was not the case for the Plains Cree. As there was within the band a balance between individual aggrandizement and social welfare, so in the external world the individual quest for status did not disrupt group military activity which supported trade systems and fed goods back into the band for the purpose of status and wel-fare. Large-scale campaigns organized by the Cree and directed toward tribal in-terests continued throughout the period. D.W. Harmon devoted a number of pages in his journal to describing the organization of a Cree campaign in 1816. He noted how they had prepared themselves all winter, collecting "bows, arrows, guns and ammunition."[45] Then, as the spring approached, the chiefs sent

[handwritten margin: war parties especifica-lly meant for status dis-play & prestige; ceremony ritualistic manners]

> ... men with presents of tobacco, to the whole tribe ... inviting them to meet at a specified place early in the spring, in general council. ... The war pipe is then lighted up, and those who are willing to become soldiers in the campaign, smoke the pipe. None are compelled to enlist but, to excite in the young men a martial spirit and to stimulate them to become his followers the war chief makes a long harangue, in which he relates the injuries, that they have received from their enemies.[46]

In 1848 Paul Kane witnessed Kee-a kee-ka-sa-coo-say, head chief of all the Cree, "travelling through all their camps to induce them to take up the tomahawk and follow him on a war expedition."[47] John Macoun, a western observer who ex-perienced those times, commented: "War parties and horse stealing parties were altogether different, and any traveller could tell the one from another at a glance. When a war party is organized the braves are mounted on their best horses, they are daubed all over with paint and depart with much ceremony. It is not so with horse stealers."[48] Edwin Denig observed that there had "been times when numerous assemblies took place including most of the nation, particularly when large war ex-peditions were about to be formed."[49]

The foregoing evidence of the persistence of large-scale campaigns indicates that Cree military activity did not become simply a status game played by aggres-sive individuals; although the military activity might have been a part of the motiva-tion of warriors in both the small and large war parties, it should not be suggested as the sole cause of war. Tribal interests, whether they were traditional positions of

[handwritten: – consolidation of the Cree nation, centralization.]

opposition to given tribes, collective revenge sorties, or the prosecution of campaigns under military alliances supporting trade systems, did not disappear. If anything, the era of the horse wars brought consolidation, not decentralization, to the Cree nation. As Edwin Denig noted, "These [Cree] like other nations, by the introduction of the horse and firearms, were enabled to hunt and locate in large bodies capable of defense and subsistence."[50]

For the Plains Cree, then, the period between 1810 and 1850 was one of cultural, and possibly even numerical, expansion. Through their contacts with other plains tribes, they acquired many of the well-known characteristics of the Plains Indians. Yet, they developed a plains culture which was peculiar to themselves and which reflected their historic experience. In the preface to his description of the Plains Cree, Denig noted, "The nation now about to be considered, together with their employments and country they inhabit, impose upon us a somewhat lengthy description from the fact that in many things they do not resemble the others."[51] Part of this difference was based on the lingering cultural memories of their woodland origin. Although they had abandoned the woodlands, they maintained the burial practices exhibited by their woods-dwelling relatives, the Ojibwa.[52] The horse and the buffalo, the two most important animals in plains life, and ceremonial objects in some plains societies, did not become special objects in the religion or the ceremonialism of the Plains Cree. However, the dog, which was both a woods and plains companion, "was an important ceremonial object, functioning as an accessory to rather than an object of ritualism."[53]

Perhaps one of the most interesting examples of Plains Cree cultural variance based on their historic eastern experience is found in art forms, specifically beadwork patterns. The classic plains pattern consisted of "a few rectangular and triangular designs for the composition of complex figures." But the Cree invariably worked in elaborate floral designs which M. Barbeau considered as having been derived from "rococo figures and ornaments of [the] Francis I period as transported to Canada."[54] As both a personal and tribal expression of heritage, the floral motif is an appropriate emblem to signify the unique experience of the Plains Cree.

It is important, however, to look forward as well as backward. In 1810 this Cree Plains experience had only sixty more years to run before their way of life was disrupted by the most catastrophic of events – the decline of the great buffalo herds and the coming of the Canadian treaty makers.

- process of cultural growth; development of particular plains lifeway; strengthening of social groups/structures; defined identity separate from other plains people – particularly in religious system and symbolism, art

The Military Chronology, 1810 to 1850

8

The need to acquire an adequate and secure supply of horses was central to the breakdown of Cree-Mandan-Hidatsa relations and the Cree-Blackfoot alliance. In both these political upheavals circumstances worked against the Cree. The choice by the Blackfoot of a Gros Ventre alliance, which secured access to the Gros Ventre horse market, and the appearance of a southeastern supply of European goods for the Missouri River tribes, cut the Cree and their Assiniboine allies off from suppliers of horses. *No Blackfoot, no middlemen position.*

The manner in which the Cree and Assiniboine reacted to this development on the northwestern plains was identical to their behaviour toward their former Mandan-Hidatsa friends. The Assiniboine led the way. In 1807, the year after the Blackfoot-Cree alliance came to a violent end, James Bird, master at Edmonton House, reviewed the situation among the tribes on the Canadian plains, laying particular stress on the behaviour of the Assiniboine: "These Stone Indians are the most useless and the most troublesome Tribe that inhabit these parts, they kill no Furs, and Horse Stealing is their trade, their Depredations never cease but are extended to all the Tribes of Natives as well as the Traders from Red River to this place."[1] The Cree followed closely the example of the Assiniboine. By 1810 raids had reached a climax, both in frequency and in success. In that year the HBC reported losing 650 horses in the Fort Edmonton area alone.[2]

The Company, although stung by their losses, remained passive. The same cannot be said for all Canadian traders, nor for the Blackfoot. In March 1810 Alexander Henry decided to make an attempt to get back his horses. He called together a Blackfoot band led by Old Painted Feather and held a council, offering them "four Kegs of Indian Rum, and one roll of Tobacco if they would go for them in a peaceable manner but they did not relish the proposal." Although it is not surprising that his scheme was rejected, Henry subsequently learned that "they had a plan of their own which had been in agitation for sometime past of being fully revenged upon the Horse Thieves, for their daily thefts that as soon as the Snow was gone off the ground, and all their young returned from War the Indians below would feel the weight of their anger." In preparation for this event, the Blackfoot "had some time ago sent Tobacco about to invite all the other different Tribes of the Slave [Blackfoot] Indians to assemble upon the Red Deer River."[3]

The slowness of the Blackfoot to take large-scale action against the Cree and Assiniboine horse thieves was caused by the fact that since 1806 they had been forced to fight a two-front war. Much of their attention during the period was directed to the enforcement of a blockade against the Snake, Kootenay and Flathead, and failing that, in making a final attempt to damage those tribes before they became sufficiently well armed to pose an offensive threat.

When the Blackfoot finally turned against the Cree and Assiniboine, the conflict became intense. In April 1810 Cree messengers circulated among the allies' camps, designating the Eagle Hills as the general rendez-vous for a summer war campaign.[4] Although this was both an expected and traditional move, the Cree had already taken decisive action which represented a significant break with the past. Somehow the Cree managed to penetrate Blackfoot territory and began to "take supplies of Arms and Ammunition"[5] to the Flathead. In 1810 an armed body of Flathead killed sixteen Piegan, causing the Blackfoot to tell the traders they would be on guard against Cree traders in the future,[6] and adding another motive, besides the punishment of horse thieves, to the Blackfoot campaign of 1810. This Cree-Flathead contact was tentative and precarious, for it could only be maintained through Blackfoot territory, but it does represent the first effort by the Cree to construct a new trade and military system for getting horses.

There was another variable in this emerging military pattern on the northwestern plains. It was introduced not by the Cree, but by the Blackfoot and their allies the Gros Ventre, and it threatened to open a third front. In 1810 the Blood and Gros Ventre Indians fell upon a party of trappers near the junction of the Yellowstone and Big Horn rivers in Crow country. They murdered some Americans and brought away "a considerable booty consisting of Goods of various kinds." The Crow were infuriated by this attack upon their traders. The following year they met the Gros Ventre on the battlefield: "During the heat of the Battle the Crow Mountain Indians called out to them, that in future, they would save them the trouble of coming to war upon them. That the ensuing Summer they would in Company with the Americans go to war upon them and find them out upon the Banks of the Saskatchewaine."[7]

This announcement sent waves of panic through the Gros Ventre tribe. They realized that there was no safety in retreat, since the Crow were numerous and aggressive. Moreover, they knew that the Cree and Assiniboine would also attack them. The Gros Ventre leaders, as they had done some fifteen years earlier in the face of a similar situation, decided on a dramatic course. Alexander Henry said that they planned to "come into our Forts [North West Company] under a pretence of Trade, and taking us unawares and unprepared to defend ourselves – to murder and plunder us of our Property, which having done they would find themselves in a state to defend themselves against their enemies."[8]

Fortunately for the traders and the Blackfoot, the Gros Ventre confided in the Piegan. The Piegan warned them that an attack on the traders would drive them away forever, leaving everyone without any means of defence, except their enemies, who would have to trade with the Americans. The Gros Ventre may have remained unconvinced by this logic, for the Piegan finally told them that if "they [Gros Ventre] fought with us [the traders] they must fight with them also."[9] This put an end to the Gros Ventre threat to the Blackfoot source of arms, but it also weakened the Gros Ventre-Blackfoot alliance. It was clear that the Gros Ventre were not a strong military ally. Within five years the Blood Indians displayed open hostility to them, preventing them from coming to the Saskatchewan posts to trade for arms.[10]

By 1811 this new, three-sided military pattern, although as yet largely uncoordinated, was clearly evident. In that year the Crow fulfilled their promise made to the Gros Ventre by marching north to engage them in battle.[11] The Cree also launched a successful attack on the Blackfoot in 1811 and the Flathead met with success in a battle with the Blackfoot in 1812.[12]

Although this new pattern was functioning to their advantage militarily, the Cree were not deriving substantial trade benefits from it. The flow of horses from the Flathead must have been limited and uncertain, owing to Blackfoot control of the trade route. There was no contact between the Cree and the horse-rich Crow except through the Mandan-Hidatsa villages. Their common antipathy to the Blackfoot had not yet drawn them into any kind of an alliance. In the face of continued Blackfoot hostilities, the Cree could do little but continue their campaigns against the Blackfoot and their horse herds.

The Blackfoot-Cree warfare continued until 1815 when a shift in Cree fortunes became evident. Early in that summer a band of Assiniboine warriors fell upon twenty tents of Sarcee and Blood Indians, killing four men and one woman.[13] This was followed in November by an ambush and the destruction of eight tents of Blood Indians by a combined force of Cree and Assiniboine.[14] In October the Cree withdrew to the junction of the South and North Branches of the Saskatchewan and prepared to defend themselves against an expected large-scale Blackfoot reprisal which never materialized.[15] The winter passed quietly and in the spring the Cree, possibly taking heart from the fact that in the previous year they had struck at will without retaliation, formed a large war party and set off for Blackfoot country.[16] James Bird, then residing at Carlton House, recorded the success of this venture: "The Southward Indians after destroying last summer a great number of Women and children of the blood Indians fled to this place to conceal themselves, and they pass the winter in this neighbourhood."[17]

Within two years the Cree, with the aid of their Assiniboine allies, had gained the upper hand. The traders seemed to realize this and feared that "if the Southward [Cree] and Stone Indians stand their ground, . . . no white Men will be permitted to go higher up this River next fall than this place [Carlton House]."[18] Although a blockade may have increased their advantage, the Cree did not do it. The events of the summer of 1818 may have made them regret that decision. In two separate battles the Cree lost three warriors and suffered twenty-three wounded while fourteen Assiniboine lost their lives; the Blackfoot sustained minor casualties.[19] That winter the Assiniboine chief, The One That Holds the Knife, toured the Cree and Assiniboine encampments, rallying martial spirits and recruiting warriors for a campaign in the summer of 1819.[20] Then, in the first week of March, without warning or explanation, "the Stone [then near Carlton House] received the Slave Indians tobacco, smoked for the purpose of making a peace with the above Tribe and also put one piece of their Tobacco in a fine painted Bladder to be sent to the Slave Indians by the first opportunity for them to smoke which signifies making Peace."[21] On 19 April a contingent of Cree and Assiniboine peacemakers from Carlton House approached Edmonton House; "a few Blackfeet arrived and peace was made."[22]

It is interesting to note that after thirteen years of continual hostilities (1806 to 1819) the Blackfoot suddenly sued for peace. Throughout this period they had not only suffered repeated blows from the Cree and Assiniboine, but they had also been compelled to fend off attacks of the Crow, Flathead, Snake and Kootenay. This move for peace probably represented an attempt by the Blackfoot to relieve themselves of some of the pressures of this three-front war. There is evidence that the Blackfoot wanted and badly needed a recess to recruit their strength. There is no doubt that these years of war had drained Blackfoot resources. James Bird noted, after the summer of warfare in 1816, "They [the plains Indians] appear to be doing very little in the fur way and our men can scarcely get sufficient Meat for their present subsistence." With the summers spent in war and winters passed in council and preparation for war, the Blackfoot stock of valuable European weapons would have been diminished. The first step the Blackfoot took toward recruitment was to order the traders to recall their buffalo hunters from Blackfoot lands. The traders realized, "The motive that Blackfoot have in view for driving away our hunters is, that by in so doing, we must apply to them for buffalo meat, for which they can make their own price."[23] If this ploy were successful, they could rebuild their firepower at an even faster rate than normal. The second step toward recruitment was the Blackfoot-Cree-Assiniboine peace.

For the Blackfoot the peace of 1819 came not a moment too soon. Bad Head, in his winter count for 1819-1820, recorded simply a "Saskina/pastsimisin" (coughing epidemic). The traders at Edmonton recorded the tragic details: "It appears from the reports of the Muddy River [Piegan] Indians the Fall Indians and the Blood Indians that the Meazles have carried off one third of their Country-men."[24]

The Cree, perhaps fearing infection, stayed clear of Blackfoot camps. It is obvious, however, that something was stirring in Cree councils. In June 1820 "a large camp of 200 Tents assembled to prepare for war but they did not go."[25] Some Cree did join a successful Assiniboine war party against the Gros Ventre in July.[26] Then on 17 August 1820 "15 Crees arrived [at Carlton House] they went away some time ago to steal horses from the Slave Indians they fell in with 10 Tents of Blackfeet Indians but being unable to get their Horses away they fired on the Tents in the night time and [say] they killed five."[27] Again it was horses that appeared to be causing the strain in this new Blackfoot-Cree accord. There is no evidence of any horse-trading between these two tribes during the term of peace. The Cree and Assiniboine battle against the Gros Ventre seems to indicate that the Cree-Blackfoot agreement excluded a Cree reconciliation with the Gros Ventre and therefore did not permit Cree entrance into the Gros Ventre–Arapaho horse market.

The troubles of the summer and autumn of 1820 were the preliminaries for the final failure of this new Cree-Blackfoot accord. Between 6 and 24 August 1821, five hundred Cree and Assiniboine warriors "fought a Battle on the South Branch River with the Slave Indians." The Blackfoot, in the spring of 1822, countered with an unexpected move. They invited the Cree to join a campaign against the tribes on the west side of the mountains. The Cree, undoubtedly fired by the thought of acquiring horses as booty, agreed to go. But on 26 February 1823 some Sarcee arrived at Edmonton House: "They inform us that 2 Cree Indians have been killed by some of the Plains or Slave tribe who are supposed to be Blackfoot – and which very likely will be the cause of war being declared between these 2 Tribes."[28]

The Assiniboine, who had not been sent the invitation, spent the summer of 1822 in warfare. Donald MacKenzie, then leading the HBC's Bow River Expedition, received a Blackfoot delegation on 3 November 1822. He was told that the Crow Indians had destroyed five Piegan families on the Belly River and that a "war party of the Stone Inds. came on the Tents of them also while the men were Hunting and massacred the whole, the party Hunting heard their firing and immediately proceeded to their Tents and found all their Families Butchered, they instantly pur-

- peace agreement was over by 1820.

sued them and Killed from Eighteen to Nineteen of them, open war being now declared by all the Slave tribes against the Stone Indians."[29]

The Assiniboine, however, were quick to mend their ways. In the spring of 1823 they made peace with the Blackfoot proper, and on 30 March 1824 the Gros Ventre reported that the Assiniboine "were negotiating about a treaty of peace with the plains tribes at that time and which has been concluded between both parties with the usual ceremonies of smoking."[30] In the autumn of 1823 the Cree, after a series of skirmishes with the Blackfoot, tried to follow the Assiniboine lead but, "after a number of fruitless Speeches on both sides, they parted no better friends than they met."[31] Another Cree attempt to make peace with the Blackfoot in April 1824 ended in failure.[32]

Throughout the Cree-Assiniboine-Blackfoot peace, the Blackfoot had been continually under attack from the Crow. It was not until the winter of 1824 that the Blackfoot could celebrate a decisive victory over them.[33] With the Cree-Blackfoot peace ended, the Blackfoot took matters firmly in hand. In the summer of 1825 a large company of Blackfoot warriors attacked the Beaver Hills Cree and destroyed "16 tents of them."[34] Then, in October they took another step which undoubtedly strengthened their efforts against the Cree. Representatives of the Blood, Piegan, Gros Ventre and Blackfoot proper crossed the mountains and made peace with the Flathead, Nez Perce and Kootenay.[35] By December they had returned and sent off a contingent in an unsuccessful search for the Cree.[36] During the summer of 1826, battles raged between these two adversaries. Then, in September the Blackfoot scored a significant victory. Chief Factor Rowand of Edmonton House reported on a "battle between our Blackfoot and their allies the Fall Indians, Blood Indians and Surcees with the Crees of the lower country . . . on the South Branch River and ten Crees with seven Blackfeet remained upon the field the Crees deserting their Lodges exposed them to the ransack of their enemies who pillaged and carried off everything that could be obtained about eighty Leather Tents become a sacrifice to their fury."[37]

Although their forces were in disarray, the Cree had not lost their ability to launch a diplomatic counter-offensive. In the month following their loss to the Blackfoot, they disclosed that they had made a "treaty with the Crow Indians . . . and that they had visited the American traders and were well received by them"[38] and, finally, that they had arranged to meet the Kootenay in council during the summer of 1827. By these moves the Cree not only placed themselves in direct contact with two suppliers of horses, but they also began to weld together an alliance against the Blackfoot. It was a determined effort to check the Blackfoot's ability to consolidate their forces on one or two of the three fronts by gaining the neutrality of their third adversary through a peace treaty.

These diplomatic moves began to pay immediate dividends. Early in February the Blackfoot retreated northward to Edmonton House. A few weeks previously, "they were attacked by a Party of Crow Mountain Indians when they received a very unpleasant *bon jour* that put an end to fifteen Blackfoot amongst whom there were three or four men of distinction . . . and they say the Crow Indians followed them to no very great distance from this Establishment our poor Indians lost upward of one hundred and sixty-five horses in this affray." In the month that followed the Gros Ventre "were again attacked by the Stone Indians" and news reached Edmonton that "fourteen Piegan of those gone to hunt beaver across the Mountains were Killed by a War Party of Crow Mountain Indians."[39]

The success of Cree diplomacy and the ensuing campaigns can be appreciated best by considering a comment on the state of the Blackfoot Confederacy by Chief Factor John Rowand: "On every side these poor devils are beset with enemies." In considering the particular case of the Blood, he determined, "It appears that these Indians imagine the source of their welfare and tranquility arises in immediately revenging attacks made upon them without considering of measures that would enable them to execute such objects effectually – their frequent failure in attempts of this Kind only aggravates the cause, and is adding fuel to the fire they would extinguish." Had he been in their place he would "adopt some domestic plan to furnish themselves with horses and to establish a peace with their neighbours the Stone Indians which would aggrandize their forces to check the enmity of the Crow Mountain Indians."[40]

There is no proof that Rowand's thoughts reached the Blood Council, but on 25 March 1827 "the Bulls back fat [a Blood Chief] invited the few Crees now here to smoke a pipe with him and his companions as a token of peace which he solicits on behalf of himself and his country men and has left Tobacco and a little weed and a piece of Buffalo back fat tied together and to be sent to the Stone Indians and Crees of Carlton." A few days later the Blood announced their determination "to carry on war with the Crow Mountain Indians."[41]

It was not only a desire to be revenged upon the Crow that drove the Blood tribe of the Blackfoot Confederacy to approach the Cree and Assiniboine with a view to peace. An important secondary reason was that their stock of horses had been drastically reduced. Rowand noted: "To deprive these people of their horses is to take from them their only riches which so many recent plunders have completely effect[ed]." By 1827 the Blood were "indifferent whether they sell their horses at extravagant prices or not the number amongst them having so much diminished which enhances their sale nearly 80 per cent."[42] The fact that the Blackfoot had that winter retreated to Edmonton House before the advancing Crow could have meant that the route to the southern horse market was blocked. The only course left to them was to re-open that route by force. The Blood may have hoped that the Cree and Assiniboine would help them.

The Blood overture of peace to the Cree and Assiniboine did not represent the wishes of the whole Confederacy, however. Just two weeks after that event a band of Blackfoot warriors left Edmonton House on an unsuccessful war expedition against the Cree. Yet, on 20 July 1827, "early in the morning four Beaver hill Crees arrive and are come for the purpose of making peace with the Slave Tribes."[43] Unfortunately, what the outcome of this visit was, whether or not these Cree peacemakers ever met with any of the tribes of the Confederacy, is not known. Only the Cree readiness to discuss peace is evident. The available sources reveal nothing of Cree movements from that point until 7 April 1828. On that day the Cree peacemakers once again arrived at Edmonton and met the Blackfoot, Blood and Sarcee under the leadership of The Feather, and "the conciliatory Pipe went round to the satisfaction of everyone."[44] An important part of the settlement was the Cree promise "not to steal their horses I have in consideration given them three."[45] A gift of three horses was small, but if it represented peace on the one hand, and Blackfoot willingness to trade their horses to the Cree on the other, both sides were probably well pleased. Finally, on 3 August 1828 the Cree made peace with the Blood who had originally taken the first step toward a reconciliation.[46]

When the news of these treaties reached Carlton House, Chief Factor Pruden recorded in the post journal the mixed reactions of the local Cree. Some were highly pleased, but there was "another party of Crees which still remain doubtful whether they will consent to Peace and these are the strongest Party."[47] The seeds of disruption seem to have been sown at the very outset of this peace.

Unlike the Cree, the Assiniboine made no reply at all to Bull Back Fat's proposal of 25 March 1827. In the autumn of 1827 Assiniboine warriors attacked an encampment of Blackfoot and Piegan families "and the latter were all destroyed excepting one man and nine women who were out gathering Plains Turnips and escaped the carnage." Shortly after that victory they discovered another Blackfoot camp, but "upon the eve of fighting Peace was made very gratifying to both Parties and they parted friends." Before their departure, however, the Assiniboine agreed to attend a further meeting that spring near Edmonton House so that a more formal and inclusive peace could be made. Early in April "forty eight Stone Indians arrived at the Blackfeet camp and made peace with them and . . . half of them returned with some Blackfoot for the Stone Indian Camp."[48] Throughout the summer and fall these exchanges of hospitality continued.

Although the Blackfoot had managed to end the warfare on their eastern flank, they failed to complete the second part of the Blood strategy – enlisting Cree and Assiniboine aid against the Crow. It is difficult to believe that the Cree would have abandoned such a horse-rich ally. Trouble caused by a shortage of horses in the Confederacy (at least among the Blood) was becoming serious. Peace with the Cree and Assiniboine could not solve the Blackfoot problem, and the Crow showed no signs of abandoning their offensive posture. If anything, they increased the tempo of their attacks. In February 1828 the Crow ambushed a Gros Ventre encampment and killed twenty-five of their warriors. They followed this with a successful attack on the Blood and Blackfoot. On 8 October 1828, a report reached Edmonton that "the Piegans have had a battle with the Crow Indians as well as the Snakes and that eighteen Americans have been killed."[49] Even an attempt to ease the Blackfoot position by making peace with the Snake, who had an adequate supply of horses, failed when the peace party led by Crow Big Foot was ambushed and totally annihilated.[50]

Since their settlement in 1828, Cree-Blackfoot relations had remained placid. Then, in August 1830 Louis Le Blanc, a Company trader, learned that a battle had "taken place between the Lower country Crees and the Blackfeet somewhere about the Eagle Creek [possibly the small river that drains the Eagle Hills]." These "Lower country Crees" were either those around Carlton House who, on hearing the news of the Blood-Cree accord of 1828, could not make up their minds whether to agree to it or not, or Cree from as far east as the Assiniboine River. With reference to this latter group, D. MacKenzie recorded in the Fort Pelly journal on 4 September 1830, "It appears they have had a dust with the Blackfeets where 13 of the latter was Killed and two of the former and some of their Horses taken."[51]

Both the Cree around Edmonton and the Blackfoot were surprised and alarmed by the news of this battle. The Cree formed large camps for their defence but they undertook no preparations for a campaign against the Blackfoot.[52] The winter of 1830–31 went by without incident. When the spring came to the plains, the Blackfoot-Cree peace appeared even stronger. Patrick Small, then in charge of Fort Pitt, recorded the arrival of "eight Blackfoot and their families; . . . they have been tented with the Crees the whole winter."[53] Joint council meetings may also have been conducted, for Small was informed by the Cree that "a great many of the Beaver Hill Crees are going to join the Blackfeet for the purpose of going to war with them on the Crow mountain Indians."[54] Although it would seem that the Cree had finally been drawn into an attack on their Crow allies, the scheme was destroyed by a series of disputes over horses between the Beaver Hills Cree and the Sarcee which continued throughout the summer and fall of 1831.[55] By the spring of 1832 the Cree had turned on the Blackfoot proper "and Killed four young men . . . owing to these Blackfeet having stole their horses."[56] Many of the Cree headed south where in September they were found camping with the Crow Indians. In October a large Cree war party moved north in search of the Blackfoot.[57] This Cree-Crow reunion would seem to have guaranteed that the Blackfoot would find no peace along their southern flank; however, another development won for them a secure and valuable military power base. This was the radical change in the temper of Blackfoot-American relations.

Since the appearance of American traders on the Missouri in the first decade of the nineteenth century, the Blackfoot had waged a relentless campaign against them. Indeed, a Blood Indian massacre of nineteen traders in 1823 became a minor international incident. American newspapers charged that "they [the Blood] were incited to these barbarous acts by the Traders of the Hudson's Bay Company."[58] There is no proof that the HBC was the guiding force behind Blackfoot aggression on the Missouri; nevertheless, it is certain that whatever disabilities the Americans had to suffer were viewed as beneficial to Company interests.

Company interests in this instance demanded that the Americans be excluded from the beaver-rich Snake country on the west side of the mountains, which the Company worked by organizing an annual trapping expedition and by encouraging the Piegan to cross the mountains in search of furs. In an effort to strengthen their hold over the Snake country, the Company supported James Bird, Jimmy Jock and Hugh Munro who, like *coureurs de bois*, lived with the various Piegan bands. George Simpson stated, "[By] their bravery and activity [they] have obtained great influence with the Piegan tribes, this influence Mr. Rowand turns to profitable account and by good management these thoughtless young men may be exceedingly useful to us not only in the way of Trade but as a means of offence or defence should the posture of affairs with America render it necessary hereafter to avail ourselves of the Services of the plains Indian tribes."[59]

Those Americans who managed to elude the Blackfoot blockade and reach Snake country found that they could not compete effectively against the British traders who brought low-priced goods in by sea. The Americans' long and unsecured supply line stretched back to St. Louis and inflated the cost of their trading goods. With these factors working for it, the HBC was, by 1827, almost the sole beneficiary of that resource area, a condition it enjoyed until 1831.

Quite unexpectedly in the spring of 1831, Blood and Blackfoot warriors crossed the Rockies and attacked the HBC Snake Country Expedition.[60] Subsequently, the Piegan sent messengers to Kenneth Mackenzie of the American Fur Company. They signed a treaty with Mackenzie and obtained a promise that a post would be established near their lands in the following year.[61]

The suddenness of these events is deceiving, for they were actually the product of a process that had begun some time earlier. By 1830 the supply of beaver both in the Snake country and around the sources of the Missouri had all but disappeared, owing to the strength of British-American competition and the thoroughness of

Blackfoot trapping. The Americans, unable to compete on the west side of the mountains, withdrew eastward, consolidated their position on the Missouri and raised the price paid for buffalo robes. The Americans had an advantage over the HBC in selling buffalo robes, since their transport route, the Missouri River, gave direct access to both the resource area and their supply base, St. Louis, and it allowed bulk shipping by steamboat. Added to these benefits was the existence of a ready home market for buffalo robes. In 1832 the American Fur Company on the Missouri traded twenty-five thousand beaver and forty to fifty thousand buffalo robes.[62] It was estimated that between 1833 and 1843 the American Fur Company traded seventy thousand robes each year while the HBC received, at most, ten thousand robes annually.[63]

The new price for buffalo, the noticeable lack of beaver, and possibly the fact that the Americans were now firmly established in the role of friendly traders rather than trader-trappers bent on an invasion of the Blackfoot homeland all brought about the reversal of traditional Blackfoot opinions of Americans. The effect on the HBC's control of the resources of the area and of the Blackfoot was dramatic. Simpson, who had been highly confident in 1827 of Rowand's ability to influence the Blackfoot, now reported: "[They] have of late been drawn to the lands of the Missouri by the high opposition prices offered in that quarter."[64] The Company's Saskatchewan district, where the Blackfoot had once traded without exception, showed a loss of £2,000 in the season 1833–34. In the same year Simpson ordered that Rocky Mountain House, the post maintained especially for the Piegan, be closed.[65] Middle Bull, a Piegan chief, reviewed this new situation in a speech to the trader in charge of Fort Mackenzie in 1833:

He hoped that the Whites would renounce their bad opinion of them, and not believe that they took their skins and furs to the English for it was evidently their (the Piegan's) own interest to be on good terms with the fort situated in their neighbourhood, the English settlements being at too great a distance; that if some of their people talked of carrying their beaver skins to the trading posts of the Hudson's Bay Company it was merely to obtain goods on lower terms.[66]

For the plains tribes, the upward revaluation of buffalo robes improved their ability to supply themselves with European goods. They were placed in a new relationship with the traders. They now supplied a valued fur as well as provisions. The result – the increased flow of European goods, especially firearms – had an immediate military consequence. For the Blackfoot, the Missouri, once only a land of Crow war parties and wandering American trappers, was now, with the construction of American posts, a military arsenal. They quickly took advantage of this fact, and subsequent military events demonstrated that they had re-established Blackfoot military power.

John Work, the HBC trader, and a band of Flathead were attacked by a war party of three hundred Blackfoot. "Nearly the whole of whom were armed with guns and well supplied with ammunition as they were enabled to keep up a brisk and continued fire upon us for upwards of five hours."[67] Work also discovered that the Blackfoot were assembling in great numbers around Fort Piegan, supplying themselves with firearms and making plans for a massive campaign against the Flathead to be undertaken that spring.[68] With the completion of their preparations, the Blackfoot struck a combined Flathead-Nez Perce camp on 19 May 1831. Three days later Warren Ferris arrived at the battlefield and recorded the events that had taken place:

They lost twelve men killed, and several severly if not mortally wounded besides upward of a thousand head of horses which were taken by the Blackfoot. The attack lasted two days, and was so obstinate at the commencement, that six or eight of the Flathead tents were cut up by their enemies and several of the latter killed in camp. There were about a thousand of the enemy; who came for the purpose of annihilating the Flatheads, root and branch. Previous to the commencement of the fray they told the Flatheads that McKenzie had supplied them with guns by the hundreds, and ammunition proportionate, and they now came with the intention of fighting, until "they should get their stomachs full."[69]

Three months after this Flathead-Blackfoot battle the Blackfoot, again a thousand strong, fell upon a small party of Kootenay, who miraculously escaped with but few casualties.[70]

The Blackfoot supplemented their military strength with a deliberate propaganda campaign. They prefaced their spring campaign against the Flathead–Nez Perce by revealing to them that Kenneth Mackenzie had supplied them with guns. In 1835 they delivered a pictograph to the Flathead. A Flathead chief interpreted its interesting contents for Warren Ferris:

Flatt-heads, take notice that peace, amity and commerce have at length been established in good faith, between the whites and our tribe; that for our benefit they have erected a fort at the three forks of the Missouri supplied with everything necessary that our comfort and safety require; that we have assembled in great numbers at the fort where a brisk trade has been opened, and that we shall henceforth remain on the headwaters of the Missouri. You will please observe that we scalped thirty of you last spring, and that we intend to serve the rest of you in the same manner. If, therefore, you consult your own interests and safety, you will not venture on our hunting grounds, but keep out of our vicinity.[71]

The events of 1831 to 1835 clearly demonstrate the commanding position that the Blackfoot were able to build from their new and profitable supply base on the

- continuous strikes by Blackfoot w/great strength.

Missouri. The Cree and Assiniboine, however, also benefited from the higher prices for buffalo robes, for by 1832 they began to take their hunts to the American Fur Company's Fort Union at the junction of the Yellowstone and Missouri rivers.[72] In the fall of 1833 they struck hard at the root of the new Blackfoot strength. Prince Maximilian, then visiting Fort McKenzie, recorded in his journal the events of the early morning of 28 August.

When we entered the court-yard of the fort, all our people were in motion, and some were firing from the roofs. On ascending it, we saw the whole prairie covered with Indians on foot and on horseback, who were firing at the fort, and on the hills were several detached bodies. About eighteen or twenty Blackfoot tents, pitched near the fort, the inmates of which had been singing and drinking the whole night, and had fallen into a deep sleep towards morning, had been surprised by 600 Assiniboins and Crees.[73]

One month later The Man That Holds the Knife, the Assiniboine chief who had led the Cree-Assiniboine warriors on that morning, reported to W. Todd at Fort Pelly that "he had been at war against the Blackfeet during Summer and had a severe Battle with them [the Blackfoot] at the American Establishment; . . . the Blackfoot saved themselves by getting into the Fort."[74]

On the northern plains the political situation had become chaotic since the breakdown of the Blackfoot-Cree peace in the spring of 1832. The cause of this was not so much the renewed Cree-Blackfoot hostilities as it was the serious disagreements which were manifest within the Blackfoot Confederacy. Since Hugh Munro's report in 1828 of fighting and horse stealing among the Confederate tribes,[75] the instability of the Confederacy had grown. Actions of the HBC, directed at winning back the Piegan and their harvest of beaver pelts, contributed to this instability. In August 1832 Chief Factor Rowand made a special trip southward in an effort to induce the Piegan to return to the Company's fold. A Company trader warned Rowand in November 1833 that "the Blackfeet and all the Slave Tribes are getting worse instead of better; they hunt less and expect more [undoubtedly a result of American prices] and are all jealous of the attention paid by us to the Piegans."[76] In December he forecast that "war will soon break out throughout the Plain [Blackfoot] tribes owing to the envious minds of their Chiefs."[77] Nine days later, on 17 December, that assessment was proven correct since "a party of Blood Indians arrived [at the Bow River post] and bring intelligence of a battle having taken place between the Piegan and Blood Indians . . . in which the Piegan camps were totally routed."[78] Additional information received at Edmonton House disclosed that the Blood "had destroyed 3 camps of the latter [Piegan] and made slaves of their women and children."[79]

The Cree were far from being unconcerned spectators to these events. As the

- Cree/Assiniboine also increased their military strength thru buffalo robe trade.
- Increased instability of plains due to problems within Blackfoot confederacy; Blackfoot jealous of Piegan-HBC relations

Confederacy was drifting toward a breakup, the Cree themselves exhibited an unusual degree of disorganization. There was an obvious difference in the position of the Cree around Edmonton and those living near Carlton House. The latter, obviously in an aggressive mood, opened the summer of 1833 by launching a successful campaign with the aid of the Assiniboine against the Blood.[80] This was followed by the vicious murder of five Piegan young men who had been invited to visit à Cree camp headed by Purapisk-at-tun, and a separate unsuccessful attack on the Piegan.[81]

The Cree of Fort Edmonton, meanwhile, seemed determined to recapture the peace which had been lost in 1832. On 16 July 1833, Black Bear, a Cree chief, "arrived [at Edmonton House] from the Blood Indian camp near the mouth of the Red Deer River where he was treated with every kindness and was assured that nothing could be more congruent to their [Blood's] feeling than having a peace established between the two nations – for which purpose they requested him to bring his tribe to their Camp but on his way he [met] with some of the war party who had killed the Piegans and so found all his hopes of effecting a peace were blasted." In disgust and anger, Black Bear returned to the Blood camp. An attempt by Old Squirrel, another Edmonton area peacemaker, to reach a settlement with the Piegan further underlined the division in the Cree community. At the beginning of a Cree-Piegan meeting held at Fort Edmonton on 29 July, "Old Squirrel got up and in the Piegan language declared that it was the Crees inhabiting the lower part of the country who always began war and that nothing could be more desirable to those of the Upper Country of which he was one than a long continuance of peace." The chief, chosen to speak for the Piegan, rose and replied that "the Indians of the Piegan, Blackfoot, Sarcees and Blood Indian tribes were always desirous to treat a Cree well but that they were such ungrateful dogs that kindness instead of making them better made them only worse they were constantly making peace and at the same time doing everything in their power to break it."[82] At the end of this imperious and insulting address the Cree, realizing the hopelessness of their aims, left.

In the midst of this dissension Black Bear, who had remained with the Blood since the disheartening failure of his peace mission, returned on 19 February 1834 to Edmonton "in search of the Crees to engage them to make war on the Piegans with the Blood Indians."[83] Unfortunately, Black Bear's work and this Cree opportunity to drive a wedge deeply into the Confederacy were lost by the action of the lower country Cree. Just two weeks after Black Bear had passed Edmonton for the Cree camps, "the 4 Blood Indians who accompanied the Little Cree [Black Bear] . . . arrived with very long faces. A war party of Stone and Beaver Hill Cree Indians amounting to about 100 attacked a Camp amounting to 30 Tents of Blood In-

✓ - Edmonton and Carlton cree did not agree on wheather make peace or fight tribes of the confedracy; sabotaged e/ group's efforts to make the inestability of confederacy even greater.

dians on the Banks of the Red Deer River."[84] Chief Factor Pruden at Carlton House learned that the war party "had killed a good many and brought off 96 Horses and 6 Women."[85] These Cree returned to Fort Pitt and spent the rest of the spring celebrating their supposed victory.[86] By the autumn the Blood recovered from the shock of their loss and met the Cree in an indecisive battle.[87]

With all hope of peace shattered, the policy of the Beaver Hill and Carlton Cree became the policy for the whole tribe. Extensive preparations in the southeast were completed in the spring of 1835. W. Todd witnessed these events and estimated that the combined Cree-Assiniboine force would number from three to four thousand warriors.[88] Even the Cree in the Edmonton area made ready. It was they who opened the campaign when their war party "about 300 in number had a battle with 22 Circies [Sarcee] Indians killed 10 of them of the Cree party 3 were killed and 10 wounded."[89]

What happened to the combined Cree-Assiniboine war party is not known. The next available evidence relates to the summer and fall of 1836. At the end of June, seventeen mounted Blood appeared at Carlton House. The trader, more familiar with the Cree tongue, had considerable difficulty communicating with them: "All that I could understand from them was that they had made Peace with the Crees and Assiniboine some where opposite to Fort Pitt." Within a month the trader received "11 Cree young men carrying the Tobacco for Peace from the Slave Indians to the Crees that reside to the Southward of this Place." Again the sources fall silent until 15 April 1837, when a report was circulated among the Cree of Carlton House that "55 Stone Indians . . . had a skirmish with the Slave Indians." The trader in charge of Carlton House concluded, "This Affair will create War again among the Plains Tribes."[90]

Although this last Assiniboine victory undoubtedly stirred within the Blackfoot a desire for revenge, the satisfaction of that urge had to be postponed, for in 1837 smallpox fell upon them. The contagion was particularly vicious in its attack on the Blackfoot and Assiniboine. One observer, profoundly affected by the suffering and death around him, wrote:

Language, however forcible, can convey but a faint idea of the scene of desolation which the country now presents. In whatever direction you turn, nothing but sad wrecks of mortality meet the eye; lodges standing on every hill, but not a streak of smoke rising from them. Not a sound can be heard to break the awful stillness, save the ominous croak of ravens, and the mournful howl of wolves fattening on the human carcasses that lie strewed around. It seems as if the very genius of desolation had stalked through the prairies, and wreaked his vengeance on everything bearing the shape of humanity.[91]

The silence of which he spoke continued throughout 1838; time was needed to reassemble the scattered bands, to mourn and to amass supplies. Once recovered, in the spring of 1839, the Blackfoot struck a weak blow at both the Assiniboine and Cree.[92]

In the south along the Missouri, the standing of the Cree-Crow alliance again worsened without clear reason. In the summer of 1838 Assiniboine warriors, led by The Man That Holds the Knife, attacked the Hidatsa, the historic ally of the Crow, but were beaten back by the villagers with the loss of sixty-four Assiniboine warriors. The Cree, perhaps realizing the folly of attacking a village, confined themselves to ambushing small parties of Crow hunters or traders.[93] The root of these Cree-Crow hostilities was, according to Edwin Denig, the Assiniboine insistence on sending out horse raiders against the large Crow herds. The result of these battles and ambushes was that the Crow not only lost horses but were also cut off, for the moment, from the supply of corn they were accustomed to receiving from their Hidatsa relatives. In 1844 the Crow, having nothing to gain from continued warfare, sued for peace and were accepted.[94] Author B. Mishkin contends that the settlement was negotiated by the Assiniboine and that the Crow were granted permission to hunt in Assiniboine territory and safe passage to the Hidatsa villages in exchange for a yearly payment of horses.[95] In that same year a peace was made between the Assiniboine and Hidatsa. Both these settlements were seen by Denig as having been laid on solid foundations.[96]

Blackfoot fortunes in this southern area had declined since their initial supremacy in the 1830s. In 1840 a Blackfoot war party of eight hundred ambushed sixty Flathead and lost sixty, although only one Flathead was killed.[97] The Crow scored a signal victory over the Blackfoot when they killed Walking Crow, a respected Blood chief in 1841.[98] The year 1845 brought fresh disasters; Father de Smet described it as a "memorable epoch in the sad annals of the Blackfoot nation. . . . In two skirmishes with the Flatheads . . . they lost 21 warriors. The Crees have carried off a great number of their horses, and twenty seven scalps. The Crows have struck them a mortal blow – fifty families, the entire band of Little Robe, were lately massacred, and 160 women and children have been led into captivity."[99] Turning to the Cree, de Smet noted that "in the preceeding year [1844] they carried off more than 600 [Blackfoot] horses."[100]

Reacting to this successful aggression on all three fronts, the Blackfoot once again turned to isolate the Cree-Assiniboine. In 1846 they made peace with the Flathead and were able to sustain the agreement for two years, when a dispute over horses disrupted it. The Blackfoot also tried to make peace with the Crow in this period but were rebuffed.[101]

In 1848 the Cree witnessed an invasion of their territory by a combined force of Piegan, Blackfoot proper, Blood, Sarcee and even some Gros Ventre Indians.

CONCLUSION

They marched as far east as Carlton House, fell upon a Cree encampment and withdrew with a significant victory.[102] There is no record that the Cree countered this blow until 1850, when a Cree war party attacked the Blackfoot near Sweetgrass Hills, killing among others Eagle Calf, a famous Blackfoot warrior.[103]

By 1850 there was no significant change in the design or functioning of the military pattern that had begun to evolve in 1810. There was still in evidence that 1850 – 180 loose alliance of tribes, Cree-Assiniboine, Crow and Flathead, which surrounded the Blackfoot on three fronts, and was bound together as much by a common antipathy to the Confederacy based on individual historic reasons as by any formal agreements. Only the Cree-Assiniboine-Crow alliance grew stronger and more formal after 1844 because it was then based not only on common opposition to the Blackfoot but also on mutually beneficial trade terms. The Cree throughout the period manifested a strong resolve and, except for a brief span in the 1830s, a singlemindedness of purpose and method. Yet, at the end of this era there was an important change taking place; it was the introduction of a new factor, a new motive for war which was added to the search to acquire horses and a horse-trading partner. This new factor was the growing scarcity of buffalo. Father de Smet was one of the first to record this development and to forecast its effects in terms of future military activity. He wrote, in the fall of 1846:

The plains where the buffalo graze are becoming more and more a desert, and at every season's hunt the different Indian tribes find themselves closer together. It is probable that the plains of the Yellowstone and Missouri and as far as the forks of the Saskatchewan . . . will be within the next dozen years the last retreat of the buffalo. The Crees, Assiniboines, the Snakes, the Bannocks, the Crows, the Blackfeet, the Aricaras and the Sioux are drawing near to these plains each year; whenever they meet, it is war to the death. These meetings must naturally become more frequent, and it is to be feared that the last of the buffalo may be disputed in a last fight between the unfortunate remnants of these unhappy tribes.[104]

The days of the buffalo wars were upon the plains Indian; the final military epoch of the Plains Cree had begun.

✓leading to renewed warfare; added to horse raids

THE BUFFALO WARS, 1850 TO 1870

IV

The Buffalo Wars'
Military Chronology

My Grandfather, we are glad to see you, and happy that you are not come in a shameful manner, for you have brought plenty of your young men with you. Be not angry with us; we are obliged to destroy you to make ourselves live. Address of welcome to buffalo entering the pound.

During the winter of 1871 the Reverend John McDougall, missionary to the Cree, met and spoke to an old Cree man travelling through the snows toward the Hand Hills. "Where are you going was my next question. Travelling for life replied the old man. Where will you find it? I again asked and back came the answer, Look yonder my grandchild; do you see a blue range of hills far away. . . . There is life said the old man. There are my people, there are buffalo; these are life to me." His people, his band and the buffalo were life to this Cree and to all plains people. The band supported the individual, applauding his deeds as a young warrior and hunter, providing a forum for his participation in social rites, and easing the poverty and burdens of his old age. The animals associated with the plains people – the dog, the horse and the buffalo – occupied "the same relation to Prairie Indians that domesticated animals and the productions of the farm and forest bear to civilized races." Although the horse was an important tool for war and hunting, it was the buffalo that was central to plains society. It provided food, skins for shelter, and clothing and bones and sinews for tools. F.G. Roe, in his special study of the buffalo, aptly concluded, "If any animal was ever designed by the hand of nature for the express purpose of supplying at one stroke nearly all the wants of an entire race, surely the buffalo was intended for the Indian."[1]

Yet, over and above the provision of subsistence and materials for tools, the great herds allowed the maintenance of an Indian way of life largely untainted by

European influences. David Thompson optimistically portrayed the land of the buffalo as "an immense track of country which the Supreme Being, the Lord of the whole Earth, has given to the Deer, and other wild animals, and to the Red Man forever, here, as his fathers of many centuries past have done, he may roam, free as the wind, but this wandering life, and the poverty of the country, prevents the labors of the Missionary to teach the sacred truths of Christianity." J. McDougall certainly agreed with at least the last part of this assessment. He wrote: "You cannot really civilize a hunter or a fisherman until you wean him from these modes of making a livelihood." Likewise, Bishop Taché admitted in 1868 that, although some plains Indians had been converted, "nearly all of them, Christian or Infidel, retain their original social customs."[2] While the buffalo were numerous, plains life was secure and provisions were bountiful, but as the herds diminished, life became hard and the traditional way that the Plains Cree had enjoyed for so many generations became less tenable.   *RESONS   FOR   DECLINE:*

This tragic development was the result of a combination of factors which can be traced back to the fur trade. Edwin Denig believed rightly that the "tendency of every fur trade is towards extinction of the game and diminishing the value of the country for hunting." Although the HBC tried to design and enforce a program of fur conservation, it did so only with limited success and only with reference to stationary woodland animals such as the beaver, otter and muskrat. He understood that "buffalo, wolves, foxes and other migratory quadrupeds could not be thus protected. Neither do we see any way of preventing their ultimate extinction except in the abandonment of the trade entirely, and reducing the natives to their primitive state of arms and ammunition." The impossibility of conserving large woodland animals caused additional pressure on the plains herds. Explorer H.Y. Hind noted that by 1860 many woods Indians had abandoned their former habitat and "now keep horses and enjoy the advantage of making the prairie and forest tributary to their wants."[3]

The decline in the size of the herds was accelerated when the American traders raised the price of buffalo robes, thereby making the buffalo a source of fur profit as well as food. In an effort to counteract this competition, the HBC also adjusted prices, and their buffalo-robe return figures indicate the resulting increase in the rate of exploitation (see Table 7).[4]

These figures, of course, do not represent the total yearly volume of robes traded, for the Missouri traders received by far the largest share of the hunts, easily ten times the HBC totals.

It is clear from the evidence of traders, missionaries and travellers that in the period between 1850 and 1870 the buffalo were disappearing. The growing scarcity of buffalo was, however, a regional phenomenon; that is, it was occurring at

TABLE 7
Selected HBC Buffalo Return Figures, 1821 to 1860

1821	200	1831	1,000	1839	7,000	1852	12,500
1823	1,500	1834	3,500	1842	12,500	1856	15,500
1829	2,000	1836	5,000	1849	7,500	1860	3,500

unequal rates in different parts of the plains, drawing the tribes into closer proximity to each other, forcing them to encroach upon the hunting grounds of others in pursuit of the buffalo.

As early as 1846, Father de Smet observed that "at every seasons hunt the different Indian tribes find themselves closer together."[5] The Cree and Assiniboine were approaching Blackfoot territory, which de Smet had forecast would be "the last retreat of the buffalo."[6] By 1862 the buffalo were gone from the Red River country,[7] and each year hunters had to travel farther west to find them.[8] The westward extension of HBC posts from the Red River indicates the wave of scarcity which moved from east to west. In 1830 Brandon House had been succeeded by Fort Ellice, built at the western end of the Qu'Appelle River, as the main pemmican-gathering post. By 1852 the Company realized that Fort Ellice itself was too far east and therefore two western outposts had to be built on the plains to bring the Company closer to the herds.[9] Dawson, assistant director of the Geological Survey of Canada, writing about the second half of the 1870s, noted the fulfillment of de Smet's prophecy. He reported that the last buffalo "are congregated in a limited area near the foot of the Rocky Mountains in the British territories [Blackfoot country] and [are] surrounded by a cordon of hungry savages."[10]

Throughout the period, occasional pockets of buffalo were discovered, which pockets broke the general pattern of east-to-west scarcity. In 1857 J. Palliser found many buffalo around the elbow of the South Branch of the Saskatchewan River, which he "accounted for by its being the neutral ground of the Crees, Assiniboine and Blackfeet none of these tribes are in the habit of resorting to its neighborhood except in war parties." Yet, the general pattern prevailed, and for the Cree and their Assiniboine allies it meant that their country, sooner than that of the Blackfoot, no longer "trembled to their tread and roar."[11]

The Cree suffered a scarcity of horses and buffalo, therefore, while their Blackfoot adversaries enjoyed the benefits of abundance. Unfortunately for the Cree, this problem could not be solved by a mixture of military and trade policies, for no Indians, although their existence depended upon the buffalo, could claim ownership of a single one. Although warfare, more particularly the invasion of Blackfoot territory, would seem to have been the sole course open to the Cree, solutions, including non-military ones, were more varied.

One of the most significant changes in Cree politics in this period between 1850 and 1870 was a new attitude toward the European, the Métis and the fur trade in general. Since their initial contact with Europeans in the late seventeenth century, the Cree had displayed pride in their "Indianness" and an independence in their political and military behaviour. It should not be assumed that Cree inclusion in the European trade system, or the obvious technological superiority of some tools brought by Europeans, placed the Europeans on a higher level in the eyes of the Cree or of any other plains tribe. Alexander Henry (the Younger) cautioned his fellow traders never "to be so vain as to believe an Indian in his heart has really any esteem for him, or suppose him his equal in wisdom or sense." Although Henry's assessment may seem somewhat cynical, missionary John West observed, "In their fancied superior knowledge they are often heard to remark when conversing with the European, 'You are almost as clever as an Indian.'" As a general rule, Indians saw themselves as the norm, and the more a European differed from the Indian, or from the trader who had been forced by the conditions of the West to adopt many Indian habits, the more ridiculous that European appeared. Hence, the scientific members of the Fleming Expedition browsing among the flora and fauna were the source of much amusement. The pinnacle of hilarity was reached when it was discovered that Fleming himself was collecting buffalo skulls, bones without marrow. This was "too much for even Indian gravity, and off he [the guide] would go into fits of laughing at the folly of white men."[12]

The Indians' confidence in their intellectual superiority was matched by a stubborn independence in political affairs. The Cree did not become unthinking pawns in the trader's race for trade and empire. Time and time again the western Cree made it clear that they would consult their own interests first. Such had been the case in their alliance with La Vérendrye, in the middleman role of the Saskatchewan Cree traders, and in Cree-Mandan-Hidatsa action against the Sioux. Possibly the most striking example of this was their answer to the efforts of North West Company traders to draw them into the dispute between the two contending fur companies over the Selkirk settlement. James Bird reported that some young Cree and Assiniboine warriors had been tempted by thoughts of easy plunder but that the chief's advice had prevailed: "You had better not interfere in the quarrels of the white people. You cannot know what party will ultimately prevail – Should you assist the weaker – You will not fail to be long punished for such interference by the conquerors, whereas tho' the party you assist should prevail, the Services You may have rendered it will soon be forgotten so that you may injure but cannot permanently benefit yourselves."[13]

Despite their ethnocentricity and political independence, relations of the Cree with the Europeans were characterized by friendliness and cooperation. Their in-

diplomacy, war and trade patterns occurred among Indians of plains before & during fur trade / Europeans rather the latter adjusted and adapted to fit into a preexisting and complex system. Indians made the fur trade work for their own relations, and Europeans had to oblige if they wanted to make a profit of the region.

terests were, with only minor exceptions, synonymous with those of the traders, and their differences were never serious enough to provoke extended or violent hostilities. In the period between 1850 and 1870 though, the depletion of the buffalo herds brought the interests of the Cree and the traders into direct opposition, and a new phase in Cree-European relations, marked by hostility (although not by violence) on the part of the Cree, began. The Cree now saw the traders and the trade system in a new light, and they were displeased by European incursions into Cree hunting grounds. This displeasure was initially directed against the Métis, whose encroachments upon Cree territory were viewed "with feelings of jealousy and enmity." Small groups of Métis were attacked, and in an effort to frustrate organized Métis hunts the Cree "set fire to the prairie about the time the brulés set out for the hunt, and by this means drove the game beyond their reach."[14]

The Cree, from their position of sole concentration upon the threat posed by the Métis trespassers, expanded their opposition to all who were not themselves Cree or allied to them. Preliminary statements against the European traders had the strong flavour of a calculated trade policy, but within a short period they began to take on a tone of desperation. By 1857 the Ojibwa, who were closely associated with the Cree, had enunciated the traditional fears of a native population in the face of the Europeans' advance: "The white man comes, looks at their [the Indians'] flowers, their trees, and their rivers; others soon follow, and they [the Indians] have nowhere a home."[15] In 1859 H.Y. Hind was invited to an important Cree council convened by Mis-tich-oos (Short-stick) in the Qu'Appelle River area. He noted: "All the speakers objected strongly to the half breeds hunting buffalo during the winter in the Plains country. They had no objection to trade with them or with the white people, but they insisted that all strangers should purchase dried meat or pemmican, and not hunt for themselves."[16] In addition to the Cree control of the trade, the leaders wished to establish their "strong objections against the Hudson's Bay Company encroaching upon the prairies [obviously a reference to the Fort Ellice outposts] and driving away the buffalo."[17] Some of the chiefs took this conclusion to its logical end and, as Hind commented, "although they acknowledged the value of firearms, they thought they were better off in olden times when they had only bows and spears and wild animals were numerous."[18] This council had decided that the Europeans and their tools were to blame for the decrease in the size of the herds and the gradual disappearance of buffalo from their lands. This was a radical departure from the previous perception of an Indian-European partnership of interests. The traders were in effect placed in the same category as others who threatened the Cree, a category which already included the Métis and the Blackfoot. In a separate council, it was decided that "they would not permit either white man or half-breeds to hunt in their country or travel through it, except for the purpose of trading for their dried meat, pemmican, skins, and robes."[19]

This council decision was not rigorously enforced. The Cree limited their actions to threats and lectures such as the one delivered to Viscount Milton and Dr. Cheadle when they were found hunting buffalo on the plains by a Cree chief in 1862.

> In your land you are, I know, great chiefs. You have abundance of blankets, tea and salt, tobacco and rum. You have splendid guns, and powder, and shot as much as you can desire. But there is one thing that you lack – you have no buffalo, and you come here to seek them. I am a great chief also. But the Great Spirit has not dealt with us alike. You he has endowed with various riches, while to me he has given the buffalo alone. Why should you visit this country to destroy the only good thing I possess, simply for your own pleasure?[20]

As well as being portrayed by the Cree as the prime cause of the decrease in the size of the herds, the HBC was charged with the responsibility for the subsequent Cree invasion of Blackfoot territory in search of buffalo and for the deaths of Cree warriors slain in the battles which were the natural result of this trespass. Some Cree felt that their charity to the European was a virtue they could no longer afford. Pee-wa-Kay-win-in, a Cree, told Isaac Cowie, a Company trader, that "in order to feed the few white people in the world, whom the Indians vastly exceeded in numbers, the allied tribes [Cree, Assiniboine and Ojibwa] had been compelled to follow the buffalo here far inside the hunting grounds of the Blackfeet. . . . In consequence two of [his] sons . . . had been slain, with fifty eight other young men in the recent battle."[21]

Although Pee-wa-Kay-win-in's estimate of the world of the European trader was certainly inaccurate, the Cree did not lose sight of the political and military realities of their situation. The council's proclamation of exclusive hunting rights, the passionate orations of the type delivered to Milton and Cheadle, and other expressions of frustration and anguish did not hide from the Cree the fact that they could not afford to break their trade relationship with the European. It is noteworthy that in speeches the Cree stressed their interest in continuing the trade. Certainly, their demand for exclusive hunting privileges represented a real desire and a concern for the resource, but they would not have fought for that principle while the Blackfoot were still a force to be reckoned with. They realized that if they were to hunt buffalo at all it would become increasingly necessary for them to visit Blackfoot territory and this they could do only as an armed force. Although they undoubtedly liked the European less, and seemed now to comprehend the destructive force of the fur trade, they needed European weapons as much, if not more, than ever. That they did not attempt to put a violent end to the trade to preserve the buffalo indicates not only a respect for European power and their own need of European weapons, but also possibly even that they knew their wealth was nearly spent, that the process of destruction was too far advanced to be halted, and that the only sensible course of action was to squeeze what benefits they could out of the remaining buffalo herds before the whole trade system collapsed. Although this might seem to exaggerate the Cree understanding of the buffalo crisis, there is evidence that at least some Cree were seeking an alternate means of subsistence, or at least a supplement to the buffalo hunt, which in itself suggests a clear understanding of the trend of events on the plains.

Adoption of this alternative marked the beginning of Plains Cree agriculture. In 1857 H.Y. Hind met a Métis, one John Spence, who was then growing corn in the Assiniboine River area, and reported that "one of his neighbors, a Cree Indian had cultivated it for four years and had not met with any failure."[22] Edwin Denig, whose writings relate to the years prior to 1855, provided evidence of what may have been, if accurate, a much more substantial, and in its details more significant, agricultural development. He noted that the Pis cha Kaw a chis, or Magpies, band of the Cree, "count 30 or 40 lodges, are stationed at Tinder Mountain, live in log cabins covered with earth, till the soil to some extent and raise considerable quantities of maize and potatoes, hunt buffalo in the winter season and get their supplies from the English posts of the interior."[23]

Three aspects of Denig's description are worthy of further note. First, the building of mud-covered, log huts was not only reminiscent of the Mandan-Hidatsa villages, but it also denoted a serious intent on the part of the inhabitants to maintain their agricultural endeavours. Second, the fact that Denig listed the Mandan-Hidatsa as a band meant that the villagers had organized themselves from scattered groups of individuals or that their involvement in agriculture had been a band decision. Either of these possibilities suggests an additional degree of purpose and permanence. Third, and possibly of greatest significance, however, is that this decision was apparently an independent Cree development, and was not induced by missionaries. Only one minister, a Mr. Pratt (Church of England), referred to the subject of Cree agriculture in this era, but he did not mention the Magpie village. He told Palliser in 1857 that "the Crees are beginning to apprehend scarcity of buffalo, and many are most anxious to try agriculture."[24] The fact that the Magpie villagers farmed in the summer and hunted in the winter would indicate an attempt to supplement an increasingly scarce supply of meat.

Although the existence of an agricultural village displayed the adaptability of the Plains Cree, it was equally evident that it involved only a minority. The remainder of the nation continued to place their hopes in the more traditional policy of war. And so the battles continued uninterrupted by the scarcity of buffalo which, along with the need to acquire horses and revenge, became a motive for war. The pattern of the loose three-sided alliance failed, and the Blackfoot Confederacy continued to show signs of instability.

It is important to note the boundary between the Cree and Blackfoot nations at the beginning of this final military era. Taking the elbow of the South Branch of the Saskatchewan as neutral ground, the Cree commanded the Canadian plains east of a line drawn from the junction of the Yellowstone and Missouri rivers to the elbow and east of a second line drawn from Edmonton (also a neutral area) to the elbow. This placed most of the Battle River and the North Branch of the Saskatchewan under Cree control. In their quest for buffalo, the Cree attempted to extend this territory far into Blackfoot country. In the beginning of this era, however, the former military pattern continued.

In the northwestern section of Cree territory, the summer of 1854 resembled so many of the summers since the end of the Cree-Blackfoot peace in 1836. "War parties of both sides [Cree and Blackfoot] kept the war path after scalps, horses and women, and many a fierce engagement resulted."[25] During the winter the Cree kept their forces in the field, ranging far to the west of Edmonton in the northern part of Piegan territory.[26] After a quiet summer in 1855, the Piegan responded to these attacks not with a war party but by sending peacemakers to Edmonton. In September "a compact was agreed upon between them and the Crees, when each went through the usual ceremony of smoking the Calumet."[27] In the month that followed, however, disturbing news of successful Cree horse-stealing raids against the Piegan reached Edmonton.[28] These raids, unlike those in previous years, did not indicate the prosecution of a separate policy on the part of the Cree of the lower country. They too were disturbed by this threat to the peace and in the spring of 1856, "the Indian Chieftain Paw pas kies from Fort Pitt accompanied by Camenacoos left here [Edmonton] this evening with a long string of Tobacco presents on a embassy to the Blackfoot Nation whom they expect to meet at the Rocky Mountain House and conciliate by the above tokens."[29] This attempt at conciliation must have been successful in expanding the peace to include all the tribes of the Confederacy; in any case, there were no reports of Cree-Blackfoot battles for another year.

When trouble came, it was again over the issue of horses. In the spring of 1857 a band of Cree and Blackfoot were camped together near the elbow of the South Branch of the Saskatchewan River. A Cree horse-stealing party of twenty-five young men silently entered the encampment and took a large number of Blackfoot horses. The Blackfoot pursued them and "at sunset they fell upon the young Crees, surro[u]nded them in the coulee in which the men encamped, and killed 17 of them on the spot with balls and arrows and by rolling large stones on them." In June the Cree struck the Sarcee in the Edmonton area and in September a party of Blood Indians reported that the Cree and Assiniboine had "stole all the mountain Piegan horses." The Piegan themselves disclosed that they had slain thirty Cree and that the Cree in general were "constantly stealing their horses." Yet, in the same month, September, "some Crees came from Mas Kie pe toon's [Broken Arm's] Camps they tell different stories about the peace" and these Cree subsequently "left for their camp with tobacco from the Blackfoot, Blood Indians and Circies," indicating that at least those three members of the Confederacy favoured a reconciliation. On 27 October Broken Arm and the Little Chief made a triumphant visit to Edmonton, accompanied by "the usual ceremony giving Horses and firing salutes."[30] The ensuing peace lasted, undisturbed, until 1860.

Along the Missouri a new element was added to the military pattern; the new element relieved the Blackfoot of much of the discomfort of Crow-Assiniboine attacks and allowed them to apply more force in the north against the Cree. From as early as the first half of the seventeenth century, the Sioux had been expanding westward, and in the eighteenth century they plagued the Cree, Assiniboine, Mandan and Hidatsa on the southeastern plains. By the 1840s a state of war existed between them and the Métis who pursued their hunts along the Red River.[31] In March 1863, after the Minnesota Uprising, the Sioux came to Fort Garry one thousand strong.[32] Despite their forbidding appearance and reputation, they remained peaceful, settling in the Portage la Prairie region. An American trader, Henry Boller, observed that further to the southwest in the late 1850s the country around the Yellowstone had been completely overrun "by strong war parties of Sioux bound against the Crow and Assiniboine."[33] Charles Larpenteur, another American, noted in 1863 that the Sioux had advanced to the Milk River in Blackfoot country.[34] With the Crow and Assiniboine distracted by the Sioux, the Cree could not expect unreserved aid from their two allies. Throughout the period there was a noticeable absence of Crow thrusts against the Blackfoot.

The Cree-Blackfoot agreement which had been reached at Edmonton in the late fall of 1857 was shattered in October 1860 when a Blackfoot chief was murdered by a Cree. For the Blackfoot, this event, although in itself a bitter occurrence, was only the final spark which ignited a growing discontent. Chief Factor Christie, in charge of the Saskatchewan district, reported that "the Blackfeet have been unbearable for the last 3 Years or more, always getting worse & worse destroying our crops, stealing our Horses and doing everything they could to annoy us, in order to provoke a quarrel so as to Kill us. They now [March 1861] threaten openly to Kill whites, Half-breeds or Crees where-ever they find them and to burn Edmonton Fort."[35] The source of their annoyance is unknown; perhaps, however, it was the growing scarcity of buffalo. The Cree, by their actions, did nothing to calm the anger of the Blackfoot. With the peace broken, the lower country Cree dispatched

Blackfoot had a free shot to fight the Cree, growing instability bc all groups were fighting for decreasing buffaloes.

a war party which fell upon a Blackfoot camp, stole their horses and killed eighteen.[36] In the spring of 1862, in full view of Fort Edmonton, they repeated their success.[37] During the summer and fall of 1862, hostilities continued unabated.

Throughout 1862 Broken Arm, the Cree peacemaker, worked diligently to change Cree policy, to prepare the way for a new and stable peace with the Blackfoot. By 7 December 1862 he was ready to meet the Blackfoot. In the company of Chief Sweet Grass and fifty Cree escorts, Broken Arm arrived that day at Edmonton and "brought a Letter from Lower Crees (Fort Pitt and Carlton) all asking for peace to be made with Blackfoot and wished to see the Blackfoot here." Chief Factor Christie "agreed to send Tobacco and a messenger to see the Blackfeet to ascertain their feelings on the matter." He also demanded that the Cree first give up their arms, a request with which the Cree complied on condition that "the Blackfeet [would] make peace and do the same." The Cree had not long to wait: on 9 December a mixed party of Blood, Blackfoot, Piegan and Sarcee answered the Cree summons. Christie continued as peacemaker. After the speeches "and promises to keep the peace [he] delivered a paper to each Chief confirming the Peace made, signed with the name of all the Chiefs present – Tobacco exchanged & sent to Slave Indian camp and Cree Camps, all parties saluted each other with a Kiss, shook hands and the Crees went off quietly at once – long may it last."[38]

The extent of Company involvement in Broken Arm's efforts before the Edmonton meeting is not clear. In the spring of 1862 Christie reported on conditions at Edmonton and concluded, "It will always be a trouble at this Fort in keeping peace between them as the Crees want payment to keep the peace."[39] The Cree realized that peace was in the Company's interest as the HBC still desired access to the Blackfoot trade. In turn the Cree were quite willing to make a profit on their military strength in that area. There is, however, no direct evidence of a Company-Cree agreement of this nature. Indeed, the Blackfoot-Cree rapprochement may simply have been the result of Broken Arm's reputation as a lover of peace for its own sake.

Several factors militated against this peace arrangement. First, the Assiniboine were not represented at these negotiations. On 18 February 1863 two Assiniboine warriors reported that two men of their tribe had just been killed by some of the Blackfoot who had been present at the Edmonton settlement.[40] Second, attendance by the Piegan at those talks concealed but did not cure the continuing instability of the Confederacy. In the late 1850s the Piegan made peace with the Flathead and allowed them to hunt on their lands. These two new allies beat off a combined Cree-Assiniboine attack deep in Blackfoot territory in 1860.[41] Within a year (by the winter of 1861–62) the value of this Flathead alliance increased as the Piegan engaged in a full-scale war with the Gros Ventre.[42] This war, and one attack in particular, heightened the dissension within the Confederacy. In the winter of 1863, the Piegan attacked a Blood-Gros Ventre encampment and destroyed four tents of Gros Ventre, including a chief.[43] By the spring of that year the Piegan and Blackfoot were no longer on speaking terms. Christie noted in the Edmonton journal "Piegans waiting patiently across the River, wont come to trouble us until the Blackfoot are off as they dont like them."[44]

The Cree, meanwhile, made good use of what proved to be but a short peace. In the autumn of 1863 it was disclosed that the Cree had once again made contact with the Kootenay and had begun to trade for horses. Broken Arm's son was one of the Cree who took part in this adventure.[45] The control over the direction of Cree policy that Broken Arm had displayed at Edmonton in December 1862 passed, however, to the more militant lower country Cree. Their first move was an attack on the Sarcee in November 1863, which was successful. On 2 January 1864 a band of Blackfoot and Sarcee came in to Edmonton and traded quickly as "they were in a hurry to be off as they expect an attack to be made on their Camp by the Crees."[46] This was followed by a Cree-Blackfoot battle late in February or early in March.[47] Then on 5 April 1864,

> . . . when Slave Indians were nearly finished trading [at Edmonton] Some Crees from Fort Pitt arrived Cumenacosse and the little pine at their head they rushed on a few who were still remaining about the fort fired several Shots, wounded one blood Indian . . . of course Blackfeet returned the compliment as best they could, however the Blackfeet ran for it and left their horses in front of the Fort the crees took advantage of the opportunity and took about a dozen of horses.[48]

Throughout the spring and summer this warfare continued with few pauses. Then, in the autumn of 1864, Broken Arm made another move for peace. On this occasion, however, there was a basic difference in his behaviour. He "determined to go with a party to the Blackfoot camp to arrange if possible, a temporary peace which might last over the winter months and thus give the Cree an opportunity to make robes and provisions for trade."[49] Broken Arm wanted a truce during which the Cree could rebuild their strength. In this he was successful, but on 18 February 1865 a freeman reported at Edmonton House "that a Cree has been Killed in the Blackfoot Camp – So much for their Peace."[50] By April the Cree were fully prepared and sent off a war party with the Assiniboine, engaged the Blackfoot in a pitched battle and withdrew with a victory.[51]

There was little that the Blackfoot could do in the face of this resolute Cree campaign, for that same spring they had been attacked by a much more deadly enemy – scarlet fever. On 24 March 1865 "L'Hereux arrived [at Edmonton] from the Blackfoot Camp brings 2 Blackfeet with him and a note from Rev. Pere La Combe

> - allowing for winter hunting; broke truce before end of season.

> - affected Blackfoot immensely at the same time as cree were preapared to fight them.

informing of great mortality among the Pagans, Bloods and Blackfeet, from scarlet fever more than 1,100 persons, men, women and children had died among the Blackfeet." Within four days of that report, one Mr. Hardisty, in command of Rocky Mountain House, sent to Edmonton an unsettling assessment of the situation in his area. The Indians were then "very hard to deal with & threatening the whites very much, blame us for the sickness, and threatened to Kill whites, an outbreak very much apprehended, Indians desperate, assistance in men and arms requested." Fortunately for the Company the Blackfoot turned their rage on the Americans in the south, killing eleven miners on the Missouri, and on the Cree or Assiniboine. In June 1865 a Blackfoot war party of eighty men "fell in with a camp of Crees or stones not certain which and killed twenty nine of them principally women and children."[52] Once again, after a series of defeats and an epidemic, the Blackfoot returned to the offensive.

The see-saw nature of the warfare in this northern area between 1850 and 1865 made it obvious that, except for the brief contact with the Kootenay, the Cree had got little benefit from their military activities. They had made no progress westward and, although they occasionally had driven the Blackfoot away from Edmonton, the Blackfoot stubbornly continued to visit that post, to the amazement of the traders.[53] It is true that Cree war parties had raided as far west as Rocky Mountain House, but these were temporary incursions from which they soon returned. Even Broken Arm's peace treaties had not produced positive benefits. Unlike the Cree-Assiniboine-Crow treaty of 1844, Broken Arm's bargains did not represent agreement on points of trade or hunting rights. The Piegan-Flathead peace and the Sioux attacks on the Crow and Assiniboine destroyed the power of the three-sided alliance of 1810 to 1850. The result was a stalemate. Realizing this, the Cree turned southward.[54]

It was toward the southern plains, bounded on the east by the line stretching from the junction of the Missouri and Yellowstone rivers to the elbow of the South Branch, that the Cree directed their attention. It was not only the bands on the North Saskatchewan who participated in these campaigns. The Cree from the southeastern plains, as well as the Swan River and Qu'Appelle River bands, had been following the westward retreat of the buffalo and also forced an entry into Blackfoot territory south of the South Branch. This southern area had been relatively peaceful between 1850 and 1865. It had been, of course, the setting of the Gros Ventre–Piegan war, but it was free of Crow war parties and there is little evidence of Cree-Assiniboine attacks on members of the Blackfoot Confederacy in the area. In the last years of this era it became the stage for violent incidents and of the final climactic battle between the Cree and the Blackfoot.

Some time between 1865 and 1868 the Cree from the Qu'Appelle area crossed

1865 – 1868 : Cree invasion of Blackfoot territory

into Blackfoot territory and advanced toward the Cypress Hills. It would be misleading to call this an invasion; it was more a heavily armed migration. The cavalcade was composed of young women, old women, children, old men, warriors and all their possessions. Nor was it solely a Cree advance, for it included "the allied Crees and Saulteaux, the semi-Stoney and Cree 'Young Dogs' of Qu'Appelle and Touchwood Hills a few English and French Métis . . . also some Assiniboines from Wood Mountain and a few from the North Saskatchewan."[55]

In 1869 Isaac Cowie visited one of these camps "consisting of three hundred and fifty large leather lodges, containing a mixed population of probably two thousand five hundred or three thousand people, of whom about five hundred were men and lads capable of waging war."[56] Although it would seem to be folly to have brought so many defenceless dependents into enemy territory, it must be remembered that these families had come to find buffalo. This was not a party of warriors, in search of plunder and glory. It was a group of people travelling for life.

The westward progress of the Cree and their buffalo-hungry allies did not go unnoticed or unopposed. In the summer of 1868 an advance guard of sixty Cree warriors visited the Cypress Hills, some one hundred and fifty miles inside Blackfoot territory. On the way back to their camp, some twenty miles to the east, they "were attacked and all killed by the Blackfoot."[57] Cree casualties continued to mount at an alarming rate. In the spring of 1869 this Cree thrust for buffalo claimed its most famous victim. On 3 April 1869 "two young fellows arrived [at Edmonton] from the Blackfoot camp and report Old Misticpictoons [Broken Arm] Killed by the Blackfoot his two sons and Grandson also about the same time."[58] The Reverend John McDougall, who had grown particularly fond of Broken Arm, sought out and recorded the circumstances of his death:

It turned out that the Crees and Blackfeet were in proximity having been forced there by the movements of the buffalo, and the Blackfeet made proposals of peace which Maskepetoon answered favourably, and himself and his son with a small party set out to arrange and ratify the compact. As he approached the camp of the Blackfeet, the latter came out to meet him with loud acclaim, and seemed very friendly, and the whole crowd of both sides sat down to quietly converse, and, as far as Maskepetoon was concerned, to smoke the pipe of peace. But while this function was going on, at a signal given by one of the Blackfeet, the massacre of the old chief and his people began, and very soon all were killed by this consummate treachery.[59]

Unfortunately, McDougall omitted from his account the location of this tragic meeting. It is known from the 29 June Edmonton journal entry that contingents of North Saskatchewan Cree and Assiniboine with their families had penetrated Blackfoot territory as far to the south as the Red Deer River.[60]

Naturally, the Cree were enraged by the murder of Broken Arm and his band of

– continuous warfare, this time expressly because of the buffalo

peacemakers. "Already while the spring was yet young, Maskepetoon's murder was being revenged and many scalps were taken."[61] In the spring that followed (1870) the Cree laid a successful ambush for the Blackfoot who were approaching Edmonton to trade. The few Blackfoot who survived fled back to their camp where they organized

> ... a large party of warriors, several hundreds in number came in to have their turn at revenge ... and when the war party came out in full force at the river they were climbing the steep banks before the fort gates with the best packs of furs to serve as shields when the bullets came. Come the bullets did, fast and furious, but as the guns were inferior and the distance considerable no one was hurt. And now that the Blackfeet took none by surprize and the fort was shut, they turned their attention to the carts.[62]

The campaign of revenge for Broken Arm's murder and the battles over the buffalo created a state of war all along the Cree-Blackfoot border.

Writing in 1911, McDougall reviewed the situation on the Canadian plains in the spring of 1870: "With the rebellion at headquarters [the Riel Resistance of 1869–70 in Red River], which was the base of supplies, tribal war around us and the fearful scourge of smallpox in sight truly the whole Saskatchewan was in a bad state." He estimated "that fully half of the native tribes perished during the season of 1870."[63] Major W.F. Butler, a British army officer, reported to A.G. Archibald, the Lieutenant Governor of Manitoba, that the Cree suffered more heavily than the Blood or Blackfoot did. Although the death toll was high, the epidemic had been like a flash of lightning, striking suddenly with deadly force and disappearing just as quickly.

By the fall of 1870 the Cree were strong enough to turn to thoughts of war. In October the Cree and their Assiniboine allies dispatched a war party of between six and eight hundred warriors led by Big Bear, Piapot, Little Mountain and Little Pine. Because Piapot was from the Southeast and Little Pine from the North Saskatchewan, the expedition appeared to be a nation-wide undertaking.[64] They hoped for a great victory and an end to the Blackfoot. Mountain Horse, a Cree interviewed after this campaign, told of a war council during which one chief rose and addressed the assembled warriors. "My children. . . . Advance and capture the Blackfoot nation, women and children. The small pox killed most of their fighters so we wont be opposed by any great number."[65] With this exhortation supporting their martial ardour, they marched westward until they found the Blood camp of Bull Back Fat and Button Chief at the junction of the Oldman and St. Mary's River, a short distance from Fort Whoop-up.[66] Having deployed their forces, the Cree chiefs ordered a full attack. At first the Cree warriors, the element of surprise giving them an edge, met with success, but soon the Blood forces were augmented by many Piegan under the leadership of Big Leg, Black Eagle and Heavy Shield. These Piegan were "armed with repeating rifles, needle guns and revolvers . . . while the Cree and Assiniboines had only old muskets, Hudson Bay fukes, and bows and arrows to depend on."[67] One young Blood warrior captured one of these old Cree muskets. "It had seven balls in it and when I fired it kicked so hard that it almost killed me. I feel that I had a more narrow escape by shooting that gun than I had with the Indians."[68] Greatly outclassed by Blood-Piegan fire power and surprised by the Piegan reinforcements, the Cree saw their attack turn into a rout. Jerry Potts, who fought with the Blood-Piegan forces, remembered that "you could fire with your eyes shut and would be sure to kill a Cree."[69] They were driven across the river and took refuge in a small wood. Some sought safety in a coulee but they were soon surrounded and put to death after a valiant, though hopeless, resistance. The Blood and Piegan then withdrew, mercifully allowing the remaining Cree and Assiniboine to return homeward. Dr. G. Kennedy, who conducted a study of the battle, concluded: "It is difficult to estimate the loss of the Crees, on account of so many being killed in the River, and their bodies swept away by the current, but it is certain that it is between two and three hundred. About forty Blackfeet were killed and fifty wounded."[70]

Throughout the winter of 1870–71 the Cree camps were filled with the mournful cries of women and children without husbands and fathers, and of old men whose sons had been slain. The weary and demoralized Cree decided on peace; in the spring they sent tobacco to the Blackfoot.[71] The summer was "a season of almost absolute rest from tribal war."[72] In the autumn the peacemakers met at the Red Deer River and concluded a formal treaty.[73] Except for occasional incidents of horse stealing, this agreement remained unbroken.

Major Butler surveyed the west in 1871. He noted: "There is not a sound in the air or on the earth; on every side lie spread the relics of a great fight waged by man against the brute creation; all is silent and deserted – the Indian and buffalo gone the settler not yet come."[74] His obituary for the buffalo was premature, for on the western plains, in Blackfoot country, the buffalo still roamed and continued to do so throughout the 1870s. On Cree lands, however, the buffalo had disappeared. Cree policy in the period between 1850 and 1870 was to attempt to expand their borders westward, but it had failed. On the plains of the North Saskatchewan, around Edmonton, the Blackfoot Confederacy, even with dissension in its ranks, had been resolute, exchanging raid for raid. The peace settlements did stall the Cree advance and allowed time for recruitment, but it did not solve the problem of the growing scarcity of buffalo. The Cree, on the southern border, made some progress into Blackfoot country, being able to hunt in large armed companies. However, their inaccurate assessment of Blackfoot losses in the epidemic of 1869–70 caused

−1870 great Cree loss against Blood-Piegan;
1871: peace agreement.

them to gamble this progress in a massive thrust designed to cripple their enemy in one stroke. They lost that gamble on the banks of the Oldman River and with it they lost any hope of extending their territories and capturing a part of the remaining herds. The initiative was then firmly in the hands of the Blackfoot. Fortunately for the Cree, the Blackfoot, after the settlement of 1871, did not, then, "in the absence of valuable game try to maintain their former extensive boundaries."[75] They allowed the Cree to wander into their territory to hunt the remaining buffalo.[76] On the sufferance of the Blackfoot, the Cree were once again able to find and hunt the buffalo. Life, for a time at least, could continue as it had for so many generations of Plains Cree.

Conclusion

By 1870 the Cree had been on the plains for nearly one hundred years; a hundred years before that they had had their first contact with Europeans. If these two centuries disclose anything about the Cree, it is that they were able to maintain an independence and integrity in the face of influence by European and also Indian rivals. Certainly, after contact the Cree changed; they became musket-carrying trappers and traders, and they moved from the woodland to the plains. This change in environment caused them to abandon the canoe in favour of the horse, the bark-covered lodge for the leather tent, and the family beaver hunt in favour of the cooperative buffalo hunt. Yet these changes did not destroy the core of the Cree nation; the ability to make and execute decisions about their interests was not, and could not have been, destroyed by new European tools or by environment-induced changes in material culture.

These Cree, both in their woodland phase and in their plains existence, participated in self-interested economic and political alliances, some of which had begun prior to contact. These alliances established the military and trade patterns which in turn determined the inland flow of European goods. Initially, the Cree and their Assiniboine allies in the southeastern and northwestern plains occupied a powerful middleman position. The coming of fur traders and the intrusion of European goods into native trade systems could not easily obliterate this pattern. The Mandan-Hidatsa trade empire admirably displayed the resilience of native value systems within which eagle feathers were valued as highly as guns were. There is little doubt that firearms secured great military victories for the armed over the unarmed. Nonetheless, as was demonstrated by the results of the Blackfoot-Cree alliance against the Snake, Flathead and Kootenay or by the Mandan-Hidatsa-Cree alliance against the Sioux, the new weapons were used in traditional patterns

rather than in creating new ones. When the distribution of firearms became universal, however, their effects were limited simply to determining the length of casualty lists. The new military power that the gun traditionally represents was used by the Cree to support their trade alliances rather than to score military victories for their own sake. Cree tribal war, which became a marked trait in their plains life and which had, always, an economic purpose, continued throughout their history.

The Plains Cree were living in a world where native people predominated. The traditional institutions of the Cree were not undermined by their relations with Europeans. Cree leaders displayed a well-developed ability to analyze their current economic and military problems and to mobilize their forces, whether they were military, economic or diplomatic, to solve these problems in a manner they hoped would be beneficial to their people. In this framework the European trader became an important, although not always the determining, variable within plains politics. The horse wars most precisely demonstrate this, since the motive for war, the underlying purpose of military and trade patterns between 1810 and 1850, was a commodity not controlled, nor even highly valued, by the European trader. Likewise, Cree participation in the most sophisticated Indian trade system, the Mandan-Hidatsa empire, was not directed solely toward improving their position in the fur trade but toward acquiring horses. The Plains Cree lived for themselves, not as European-organized appendages of an alien trade system.

By 1870 the Plains Cree had experienced a succession of military and trade crises, the breakdown of the Blackfoot and Mandan-Hidatsa alliances being the most important. Each time, the Cree reorganized their system of alliances, as in their bargain with the Crow and with the Flathead-Kootenay forces, in an attempt to recapture lost military and trade advantages. They developed a solid diplomatic tradition, and in their long warfare with the Blackfoot, they also developed a fine military record. Their flexible band system and the status system, with its focus on generosity and valour, produced an inner strength which allowed for the absorption of the shocks of epidemics and defeats and guaranteed the much-needed martial and entrepreneurial spirit.

After 1870, however, the Cree faced a crisis for which they had no experience. The buffalo had left their lands, and even though the Blackfoot, after the peace of 1871, allowed them to trespass and to hunt among the remaining herds, it was only a matter of time before the buffalo disappeared altogether from the plains, before the end of plains life was in full view, before the system of reserves divided them from their wanderings. When the end finally came, as it did in 1879, it was heralded by a tragic cry which went up and echoed across the plains.[1]

My father, have pity on me!
I have nothing to eat,
I am dying of thirst –
Everything is gone!

Turning to face the east, the Cree could see the emptiness of their lands. The great herds now ran only in their memories. All that was real was the approaching European and the strange confinement of the reserve.

If there is a tragedy in Plains Cree history, it is not that a growing dependence on white influences caused the society to crumble; rather, it is that Plains Cree society, or at least the Cree ability to organize on economic and military lines, remained remarkably unchanged, outliving the herds upon which the society physically existed. What was led into the bondage of the reserves was not the ruin of a political and social system, but rather a healthy organism which had taken root and grown strong on the plains. The fate of the Plains Cree nation followed that of the buffalo – not to death, but into a white man's pound, the reserve.

did not represent an all-encompassing force; rather they were one more player in an allready complex system.

Bibliography

PRIMARY SOURCES

1 Hudson's Bay Company Records

a) POST JOURNALS

Post	Reel	Dates
Bow Fort	IM16	1833–1834
Bow River Expedition	IM20	1822–1823
Buckingham House	IM18	1792–1799
Brandon House	IM16	1793–1795
	IM17	1795–1819
		1828–1830
Carlton House (Assiniboine)	IM20	1795–1800
Carlton House (Saskatchewan)	IM18	1795–1796
	IM19	1797–1798
		1815–1839
Chesterfield House	IM20	1799–1802
Cumberland House	IM38	1783–1784
	IM39	1784–1795
Fort Dauphin	IM41	1795–1796
		1820–1821
Edmonton	IM49	1798–1825
	IM50	1826–1829
		1832–1833
		1854–1871
Fort Ellice	IM51	1793–1794
		1812–1813

Post	*Reel*	*Dates*
		1822–1823
		1858–1865
	IM52	1865–1869
Hudson House (Upper)	IM63	1782–1783
Island House	IM65	1801–1802
Manchester House	IM73	1786–1793
Nippoewin House	IM102	1784–1785
Fort Pelly	IM116	1793–1797
	IM117	1797–1800
		1818–1838
		1854–1857
Pembina	IM117	1808–1813
Red Deer River (Swan River)	IM119	1812–1813
Red Lake	IM119	1790–1792
Rocky Mountain House	IM123	1828–1830
		1836–1837
		1866–1868
Setting River	IM131	1798–1799
Somerset House	IM143	1794–1796
South Branch House	IM143	1787–1791
	IM144	1792–1794
Windsor House	IM153	1799–1800

b) OTHER

Reel	*Document*	*Dates*
Reel 3M44	Governor Simpson Official Reports to the Governor and Committee in London	1826–1829
Reel 3M45	Governor Simpson Official Reports	1832–1839
Reel 3M46	Governor Simpson Official Reports	1839–1843
Reel 195	London Inward Correspondence from Governors of the Hudson's Bay Company's Territories	1823–1832
IM812–813	District Fur Returns	1821–1892
IM917–934	Northern Department Inventories	1821–1867
IM943–944	Northern Department Inventories	1839–1844

2 Fur Trade Manuscripts

Manuscript Number	*Document*	*Dates*
M.G. 18 D5A	Journal of Anthony Henday	1754–1755
M.G. 18 D5B	Journal of Matthew Cocking	1772
M.G. 19 A13	A. Henry's Journey, Lake Superior to the Pacific Ocean	1799–1816
M.G. 19 A19	Journal of Sir Alexander Mackenzie, Journey from Lake Athabaska to the Artic Sea	
M.G. 19 B4	Sketch of the Fur Trade of Canada, W. McGillivray	1809
M.G. 19 C1, Vol. 1	Journal of Charles Chaboillez	1797–1798
M.G. 19 C1, Vol. 3	Journal of Missouri River F.A. Laroque	1804–1805
M.G. 19 C1, No. 1	Journal at Rivière Rouge	1798–1799
M.G. 19 C1, No. 4	Journal of W. McGillivray, Esq.	1789–1790
M.G. 19 C1, No. 5	Journal of William McGillvray – English River	n.d.
M.G. 19 C1, No. 11	Journal at Lac LaPluie	1804–1805
M.G. 19 C1, No. 12	Journal Lac St. Croix	1804–1805
M.G. 19 C1, No. 14	Journal of the Rocky Mountain Fort	1799–1800
M.G. 19 C1, No. 19	Correspondence of C. Mackenzie, J. McGillivray and R. Mackenzie	1810–1820
M.G. 19 C, Vol. 4	Some account of the Department of Fon Du Lac or Mississippi by George Henry Monk	1807
M.G. 19 C2, No. 4	Aeneas McDonnell – North West Indians	1807–1808
M.G. 19 C2, No. 5a	Journal of John MacDonnell	1793–1795
M.G. 19 C2, No. 5b	The Red River by John McDonnell of the North West Company	1793–1797
M.G. 19 C2, No. 6	An account of the Athabaska Indians by a partner of the North West Company	
M.G. 19 C2, No. 9	Account of the Missouri Indians, Charles McKenzie	1804
M.G. 21–15	J. Carver – Journal of the Travels of Captain Jonathon Carver from Michilimackinac to	

Manuscript Number	*Document*	*Dates*
	the Country of the Nadawesie or Sioux from August the 12th 1766 to August 30, 1767	

PUBLISHED PRIMARY SOURCES

Abel, A.H. *Chardon's Journal at Fort Clark 1834–1839.* University of South Dakota: Published under the auspices of the Superintendent, Department of History, 1932.

Back, G. *Narrative of the Arctic Land Expedition to the Mouth of the Great Fish River and along the Shores of the Arctic Ocean in the Years 1833, 1834, 1835.* Facsimile reprint. Edmonton: M.G. Hurtig Ltd., 1970.

Bain, J., ed. *Travels and Adventures in Canada and the Indian Territories between the Years 1760 and 1776 by Alexander Henry Fur Trader.* Toronto: G.H. Morang and Company, 1908.

Ballantyne, R.M. *Hudson Bay or Everyday Life in the Wilds of North America.* London, Edinburgh and New York: Thomas Nelson and Sons Ltd., 1916.

Boller, H.A. *Among the Indians – Eight Years in the Far West 1858–1866.* Chicago: R.R. Donnelley and Sons Company, 1959.

British Parliamentary Papers, 1858, Report from the Select Committee on the State of the British Possessions in North America which are under the Administration of the Hudson's Bay Company with Minutes of Evidence. Irish University Press Series, 1969.

Brymner, D., ed. *Memoir or Summary Journal of the Expedition of Jacques Repentigny Legardeur de Saint Pierre, Knight of the Royal Order of Saint Louis, Captain of a Company of Troops Detached from the Marine in Canada, Charged with the Discovery of the Western Sea, 1751.* Ottawa: Public Archives Report, 1886.

Butler, Major W.F. *The Great Lone Land: A Narrative of Travel and Adventure in the North West of America.* London: S. Law, Marston and Rivington, 1872.

Burpee, L.J., ed. *Journals and Letters of Pierre Gaultier de Varennes De La Vérendrye and His Sons.* The Champlain Society, vol. 16. Toronto, 1927.

_____. *Journal of Matthew Cocking from York Factory to the Blackfeet Country, 1772–1773.* Royal Society of Canada Proceedings and Transactions, 3rd. ser., vol. 2.

Catlin, G. *Letters and Notes on the Manners, Customs and Conditions of the North American Indians Written during Eight Years' Travel amongst the Wildest Tribes of Indians in North America, 1832–1839.* 2 vols. Piccadilly: G. Catlin, 1841.

_____. *O-KEE PA: A Religious Ceremony and Other Customs of the Mandans.* London: Trubner and Company, 1867.

Chittenden, H.M. and Richardson, A.T. *Father De Smet's Life and Travels among the North American Indians.* New York: Francis Harper, 1905.

Cowie, I. *The Company of Adventurers: A Narrative of Seven Years in the Service of the Hudson's Bay Company during 1867–1874.* Toronto: William Briggs, 1913.

Cox, R. *Adventures on the Columbia River including the Narrative of a Residence of Six Years on the Western Side of the Rocky Mountains among Various Tribes of Indians Hitherto Unknown: Together with a Journey across the American Continent.* New York: J. and J. Harper, 1832.

Dempsey, H.A. *A Blackfoot Winter Count.* Calgary: Glenbow Foundation, 1965.

Denig, E. *Five Indian Tribes of the Upper Missouri*. Reprint. Norman: University of Oklahoma Press, 1969.

Doughty, A. and C. Martin, eds. *The Kelsey Papers*. Ottawa: The Public Archives of Canada and the Public Record Office of Northern Ireland, 1929.

Ferris, W.A. *Life in the Rocky Mountains 1830–1835*. Reprint. Salt Lake City: Rocky Mountain Bookshop, 1940.

Flandrau, G., ed. *The Vérendrye Overland Quest of the Pacific*. Reprinted from the Quarterly of the Oregon Historical Society 16, no. 2 (June 1925).

Fleming, R., II., ed. *Minutes of Council – Northern Department of Rupert's Land 1821–1831*. Hudson's Bay Record Society, vol. 3. Toronto, 1940.

Franklin, J. A *Narrative of a Journey to the Shores of the Polar Sea in the Years 1819, 1820, 1821 and 1822*. Facsimile reprint. Edmonton: M.G. Hurtig Ltd., 1969.

Gates, C.M. *Five Fur Traders of the North West*. St. Paul: Minnesota Historical Society, 1965.

Grant, G.M. *Ocean to Ocean – Sandford Fleming's Expedition through Canada in 1872*. Facsimile reprint. Toronto: Coles Publishing Company, 1970.

Hind, H.Y. *Narrative of the Canadian Red River Exploring Expedition of 1857 and of the Assiniboine and Saskatchewan Expedition of 1858*. 2 vols. London: Longman, Green, Longman and Roberts, 1860.

James, E., ed. *A Narrative of Captivity and Adventure of John Tanner during Thirty Years Residence among the Indians in the Interior of North America*. Minneapolis: Ross and Haines Inc., 1956.

Johnson, A.M., ed. *Saskatchewan Journals and Correspondence 1795–1802*. Hudson's Bay Record Society, vol. 26. London, 1967.

Johnston, A. *The Battle at Belly River: Stories of the Last Great Indian Battle*. Lethbridge: Historical Society of Alberta, 1966.

Kane, P. *Wanderings of an Artist*. Facsimile reprint. Edmonton: M.G. Hurtig, 1968.

Du Lac, M. Perrin. *Travels through the Two Louisianas and among the Savage Nations of the Missouri*. London: Richard Phillips, 1807.

Lamb, W.K., ed. *Sixteen Years in the Indian Country, the Journal of Daniel William Harmon, 1800–1816*. Toronto: Macmillan of Canada, 1957.

_____. *The Letters and Journals of Simon Fraser*. Toronto: Macmillan of Canada, 1960.

_____. *Gabriel Franchère, Journal of a Voyage on the North West Coast of North America during the Years 1811, 1812, 1813 and 1814*. The Champlain Society, vol. 45. Toronto, 1969.

Larpenteur, C. *Forty Years a Fur Trader on the Upper Missouri*. Reprint. Chicago: R.R. Donnelley and Sons Company, 1933.

Lewis, Cpt., and Cpt. Clark. *History of the Expedition under the Command of Captains Lewis and Clark to the Sources of the Missouri, across the Rocky Mountains, down the Columbia River to the Pacific in 1804–1806*. 3 vols. Reprint. Toronto: G.N. Morang and Company, n.d.

Louis, W.S., P.C. Phillips, eds. *The Journal of John Work*. Toronto: The Arthur H. Clark Company, 1923.

McDougall, J. *Forest, Lake and Prairie*. Toronto: William Briggs, 1910.

_____. *Saddle, Sled and Snowshoe*. Toronto: The Ryerson Press, n.d.

_____. *Pathfinding on the Plain and Prairie: Stirring Scenes of Life in the Canadian North-West*. Toronto: William Briggs, 1898.

_____. *In the Days of the Red River Rebellion*. Toronto: William Briggs, 1911.

_____. *On Western Trails in the Early Seventies.* Toronto: William Briggs, 1911.

_____. *Opening the Great West.* Calgary: Glenbow-Alberta Institute, 1970.

Mackenzie, A. *Voyages from Montreal through the Continent of North America.* Reprint. Toronto: G.N. Morang and Company, 1904.

McLean, J. *Notes of Twenty-five Years Service in the Hudson's Bay Territory.* London: Richard Bentley, 1849.

Milton, Viscount, and W.B. Cheadle. *The North West Passage By Land – Being the Narrative of an Expedition from the Atlantic to the Pacific.* Facsimile reprint. Toronto: Coles Publishing Company, 1970.

Moberly, H.J. *When Fur Was King.* London and Toronto: J.M. Dent and Sons Ltd., 1929.

Morton, A.S., ed. *The Journal of Duncan McGillivray of the North West Company at Fort George on the Saskatchewan, 1794–1795.* Toronto: Macmillan of Canada, 1929.

Odgen, P.S. *Traits of American-Indian Life and Character by a Fur Trader.* London: Smith, Elder and Company, 1853.

Palliser, J. *The Solitary Hunter; or, Sporting Adventures in the Prairies.* London: Routledge, Warne and Routledge, 1860.

Parker, S. *A Journey beyond the Rocky Mountains in 1835, 1836 and 1837.* Edinburgh: William and Robert Chambers, 1841.

Rich, E.E., ed. *James Isham's Observations on Hudson's Bay, 1734, and Notes and Observations on a Book Entitled "A Voyage to Hudson's Bay in the Dobbs Galley 1749."* The Champlain Society, HBC ser., vol. 12. Toronto, 1949.

_____. *Cumberland House Journals and Inland Journal 1775–1779.* The Hudson's Bay Record Society, 1st ser., vol. 14. London, 1951.

_____. *Cumberland House Journals and Inland Journal 1779–1782.* The Hudson's Bay Record Society, 2nd ser., vol. 15. London, 1952.

Robert, Major R. *A Concise Account of North America, 1765.* New York: Johnson Reprint Corporation, S.R. Publishers Ltd., 1966.

Ross, A. *The Fur Hunters of the Far West: A Narrative of Adventures in the Oregon and Rocky Mountains.* 2 vols. London: Smith, Elder and Company, 1855.

Ryerson, John. *Hudson's Bay or A Missionary Tour in the Territory of the Hon. Hudson's Bay Company.* Toronto: G.R. Sanderson, 1855.

Sheppe, W., ed. *First Man West – A. Mackenzie's Account of His Expedition across North America to the Pacific in 1793.* Berkeley: University of California Press, 1962.

Spry, I.M., ed. *The Papers of the Palliser Expedition 1857–1860.* The Champlain Society, vol. 44. Toronto, 1968.

Taché, Mgr., Bishop of St. Boniface. *Sketch of the North-West of America.* Montreal: John Lovell, 1870.

Thwaites, R.G., ed. *Journal of a Voyage up the River Missouri, Performed in 1811, by H.M. Brackenbridge.* Cleveland: The Arthur H. Clark Company, 1904.

_____. *Travels in the Interior of America, 1809, 1810 and 1811, by John Bradbury.* Cleveland: The Arthur H. Clark Company, 1904.

_____. *Journal of Travels in the Arkansas Territory during the Year 1810 with Occasional Observations on the Manners of the Aboriginies by T. Nuttall.* Cleveland: The Arthur H. Clark Company, 1905.

_____. *Travels in the Interior of North America by Maximilian, Prince of Wied,* 3 vols. Cleveland: Arthur H. Clark Company, 1905.

_____. *Letters and Sketches – Father Pierre Jean de Smet*. Cleveland: The Arthur H. Clark Company, 1905.

Tyrrell, J.B., ed. *Journals of Samuel Hearne and Philip Turnor*. The Champlain Society, vol. 21. Toronto, 1934.

_____. *David Thompson's Narrative*. New York: Greenwood Press, 1968.

Umfreville, E. *The Present State of Hudson's Bay*. Facsimile reprint, with an introduction by W.S. Wallace. Toronto: The Ryerson Press, 1929.

Wallace, W.S., ed. *Documents Relating to the North West Company*. The Champlain Society, vol. 22. Toronto, 1934.

West, J. *The Substance of a Journal during a Residence at the Red River Colony, British North America, in the Years 1820–1823*. Facsimile reprint. Vancouver: The Alcuin Society, 1967.

Williams, G., ed. *Andrew Graham's Observations on Hudson's Bay 1767–1791*. The Hudson's Bay Record Society, vol. 27. London, 1969.

Wood, W.R., and T.D. Thiessen, eds. *Early Fur Trade on the Northern Plains*. Norman: University of Oklahoma Press, 1985.

Young, E.R. *By Canoe and Dog Train among the Cree and Saulteau Indians*. Toronto: William Briggs, n.d.

_____. *Stories from Indian Wigwams and Northern Campfires*. Facsimile reprint. Toronto: Coles Publishing Company, 1970.

SECONDARY SOURCES

Arthur, G. "A Re-Analysis of the Early Historic Plains Indian Bison Drive." In *Bison Procurement and Utilization: A Symposium*, edited by L.B. Davis and M. Wilson, *Plains Anthropologist*, no. 14, pt. 2, 1978.

Barbeau, M. *Indian Days in the Canadian Rockies*. Toronto: Macmillan of Canada, 1923.

_____. "The Origin of Floral and Other Designs among the Canadian and Neighboring Indians." *Proceedings of the 23rd International Congress of Americanists*. New York: 1928.

Barbeau, M., and G. Melvin. *The Indian Speaks*. Toronto: Macmillan of Canada, 1943.

Billington, R.A. *Soldier and Brave*. New York, Evanston, and London: Harper and Row, 1963.

Black, N.F. *History of the Saskatchewan and the Old North West*. Regina: North West Historical Company, 1913.

Bloomfield, L. *Plains Cree Texts*. New York: G.E. Steckert, agent, 1934. [Original edition issued as vol. 16 of the Publications of the American Ethnology Society.]

Bond, J.W. *Minnesota and its Resources*. St. Paul: Redfield, 1853.

Bryce, G. *The Remarkable History of the Hudson's Bay Company*. Toronto: William Briggs, 1900.

Bushnell, D.I. *Burials of the Algonquian, Siouan and Caddoan Tribes West of the Mississippi*. Publications of the Bureau of American Ethnology, bulletin no. 83. Washington, D.C.: Smithsonian Institution, 1927.

Chittenden, H.M. *The American Fur Trade of the Far West*, 2 vols. Stanford: Academic Reprints, 1954.

Dawson, G.M. "Sketches of the Past and Present Condition of the Indians of Canada." Reprint from the *Canadian Naturalist* 9, no. 3 (1923).

Dempsey, H.A. *Big Bear.* Vancouver, Toronto: Douglas and McIntyre, 1984.

Dobyns, H.F. *Native American Demography: A Bibliography.* Bloomington: Indiana University Press, 1976.

_____. *Their Number became Thinned: Native American Population Dynamics in Eastern North America.* Knoxville: University of Tennessee Press, 1983.

Dorsey, J.O. "Siouan Sociology." *American Bureau of Ethnology, Annual Report for 1893–1894.*

Drake, S.G. *The Book of the Indians or, Biography and History of the Indians of North America from its First Discovery to the Year 1841.* Boston: Benjamin Mussey, 1845.

Driver, H.E. *The Indians of North America.* Chicago and London: The University of Chicago Press, 1969.

Eggan, F. "The Cheyenne and the Arapaho in the Perspective of the Plains Ecology and Society." In *The American Indian: Perspectives for the Study of Social Change.* Chicago: Aldine Publishing Company, 1966.

Ewers, J.C. *Indian Life on the Upper Missouri.* Norman: University of Oklahoma Press, 1968.

_____. *The Horse in Blackfoot Indian Culture with Comparative Material from Other Western Tribes.* Publications of the American Bureau of Ethnology, bulletin no. 159. Washington, D.C.: Government Printing Office, 1969.

Francis, D., T. Morantz. *Partners in Fur.* Montreal: McGill-Queen's University Press, 1983.

Gilmore, M.R. "Uses of Plants by the Indians of the Missouri River Region." *American Bureau of Ethnology, Annual Report for 1911–1912.*

Goodwill, J., and N. Sluman. *John Tootoosis.* Winnipeg: Pemmican Publications, 1984.

Hlady, W.M. *Indian Migration in Manitoba and the West.* Historical and Scientific Society of Manitoba Transactions, 3rd

ser., no. 17 (1960–1961).

_____. "Southeastern Manitoba Resurveyed." In *Ten Thousand Years' Archaeology in Manitoba,* edited by W.M. Hlady. Winnipeg: Manitoba Archaeological Society, 1970.

Hodge, F.W. "Handbook of the Indians of Canada." Reprint from *Handbook of American Indians North of Mexico.* Publications of the Bureau of American Ethnology, bulletin no 30. Ottawa, 1913.

Hyde, G.E. *Indians of the High Plains.* Norman: University of Oklahoma Press, 1959.

Innis, H.A. *The Fur Trade in Canada.* Toronto: University of Toronto Press, 1967.

Jackson, J.J. "Brandon House and the Mandan Connection." *North Dakota History* 49 (1982).

Jacobson, R.B., and J.L. Eighmy. "A Mathematical Theory of Horse Adoption on the North American Plains." *Plains Anthropologist* 25, no. 87 (1980).

Jenks, A.E. "The Wild Rice Gatherers of the Upper Lakes – A Study in American Primitive Economics." *American Bureau of Ethnology, Annual Report for 1897–1898.*

Jenness, D. *The Indians of Canada.* Ottawa: Publications of the National Museum of Canada, 1960.

_____. *The Sarcee Indians of Alberta.* Ottawa: Publications of the National Museum of Canada, n.d.

Jenness, E. *The Indian Tribes of Canada.* Toronto: The Ryerson Press, 1933.

Kay, J. "The Fur Trade and Native American Population Growth." *Ethnohistory* 31, no. 4 (1984).

Krech, S. *The Subarctic Fur Trade: Native Social and Economic Adaptations.* Vancouver: University of British Columbia Press, 1984.

Kroeber, A.L. "The Ceremonial Organization of the Plains Indians of North America."

Proceedings of the 15th International Congress of Americanists II. Quebec, 1906.

Lewis, O. *The Effects of White Contact upon Blackfoot Culture with Special Reference to the Role of the Fur Trade.* New York: J.J. Augustin, 1942.

McGee, W.J. "The Siouan Indians: A Preliminary Sketch." *American Bureau of Ethnology, Annual Report for 1893–1894.*

Mackay, D. *The Honourable Company.* Toronto: McClelland and Stewart Ltd., 1966.

McLean, J. *The Indians, their Manners and Customs.* Facsimile reprint. Toronto: Coles Publishing Company, 1970.

———. *Canadian Savage Folk – the Native Tribes of Canada.* Toronto: William Briggs, 1896.

Macoun, J. *Manitoba and the Great North-West.* Guelph: The World Publishing Company, 1882.

Mandelbaum, D.G. *The Plains Cree.* Anthropological Papers, American Museum of Natural History, vol. 37, pt 2. New York, 1940.

Martin, C. *Keepers of the Game.* Los Angeles: University of California Press, 1978.

Mishkin, B. *Rank and Warfare among the Plains Indians.* Seattle and London: University of Washington Press, 1940.

Mooney, J. "The Ghost Dance Religion and the Sioux Outbreak of 1890." *American Bureau of Ethnology, Annual Report for 1892–1893.*

Morton, A.S. *A History of the Canadian West to 1870–1871.* Toronto and New York: Thomas Nelson and Sons Ltd., 1939.

Oliver, S. *Ecology and Cultural Continuity as Contributing Factors in the Social Organization of the Plains Indians.* Berkeley: University of California Press, 1962.

Osburn, A.J. "Ecological Aspects of Equestrian Adaptations in aboriginal North America." *American Anthropologist* (1985).

Patterson, E.P. *The Canadian Indian: A History since 1500.* Don Mills: Collier-Macmillan Canada Ltd., 1972.

Powell, J.W. "Linguistic Families of America North of Mexico." *American Bureau of Ethnology, Annual Report for 1885–1886.*

Rau, C. "Ancient Aboriginal Trade in North America." Reprint from *Report of the Smithsonian Institution for 1872.* Washington: Government Printing Office, 1873.

Ray, A.J. *Indians in the Fur Trade.* Toronto: University of Toronto Press, 1974.

———. "Fur Trade History as an Aspect of Native History." In *One Century Later,* edited by I. Getty and D. Smith. Vancouver: University of British Columbia Press, 1978.

Rich, E.E. *Hudson's Bay Company 1670–1870.* 3 vols. Toronto: McClelland and Stewart Ltd., 1960.

———. "Trade Habits and Economic Motivation among the Indians of North America." *Canadian Journal of Economics and Political Science* 26 (February 1960).

———. *The Fur Trade and the Northwest to 1857.* Toronto: McClelland and Stewart Ltd., 1967.

Roe, F.G. "From Dogs to Horses among the Western Indian Tribes." *Proceedings and Transactions of the Royal Society of Canada,* 3rd ser., vol. 33, sect. 2 (1939).

———. *The North American Buffalo – A Critical Study of the Species in its Wild State.* Toronto: University of Toronto Press, 1951.

Schoolcraft, H.R. *Historical and Statistical Information Respecting the History, Condition and Prospects of the Indian Tribes of the United States.* 6 vols. Philadelphia: Lippincott, Grambo and Company, 1851–1857.

Sharrock, S.R. "Cree, Cree-Assiniboine, and Assiniboines: Inter-Ethnic Social Organization on the Far Northern Plains." *Ethnohistory* 21 (1974).

Swanton, J.R. *The Indian Tribes of North America.* Publications of the American Bureau of Ethnology, bulletin no. 145. Washington, 1952.

Wilson, C.H. "An Inquiry into the Nature of Plains Indians Cultural Development." *American Anthropologist* 65 (1963).

Wissler, C. "Diffusion of Culture in the Plains of North America." *Proceedings of the 15th International Congress of Americanists.* 2 vols. Quebec, 1906, II, 39.

_____. *North American Indians of the Plains.* New York: Museum of Natural History, 1912.

Notes

CHAPTER 1

1 D.G. Mandelbaum, *The Plains Cree,* Anthropological Papers, American Museum of Natural History, vol. 37, pt. 2 (New York, 1940), 172; and A.J. Ray, *Indians in the Fur Trade* (Toronto: University of Toronto Press, 1974), 12.

2 H.A. Innis, *The Fur Trade in Canada* (Toronto: University of Toronto Press, 1967), 46; and Ray, *Indians in the Fur Trade,* 13.

3 A. Mackenzie, *Voyages from Montreal through the Continent of North America* (reprint, Toronto: G.N. Morang and Company, 1904), cxix. To understand the catholic nature of Cree-Assiniboine relations which extended far beyond military and economic alliance, see S.R. Sharrock, "Cree, Cree-Assiniboine, and Assiniboines: Inter-ethnic Social Organization on the Far Northern Plains," *Ethnohistory* 21 (1974): 95–122.

4 For Cree and Assiniboine middleman behaviour, their control of access to the Bay and their western expansion, see: Ray, *Indians in the Fur Trade,* 19–23; 55–61.

5 See Chapter 2 for a discussion of Cree history in the Red River area.

6 The pervasive nature of this error can be seen by reference to such works as: E.P. Patterson, *The Canadian Indian: A History since 1500* (Don Mills: Collier-Macmillan Canada Ltd., 1972), 91; P. Kane, *Wanderings of an Artist* (facsimile reprint, Edmonton: M.G. Hurtig, 1968), 77; W.M. Hlady, *Indian Migrations in Manitoba and the West* (Historical and Scientific Society of Manitoba Transactions, 3rd ser., no. 17, 1960–1961), 30; and F.W. Hodge, "Handbook of the Indians of Canada," in *Handbook of American Indians North of Mexico,* Publications of the Bureau of American Ethnology, bulletin no. 30 (reprint, Ottawa, 1913).

7 These Snake are known more properly as the Shoshone. See: J.C. Ewers, *Indian Life on the Missouri* (Norman: University of Oklahoma Press, 1968), 11; and J.B. Tyrrell, ed., *David Thompson's Narrative* (New York: Greenwood Press, 1968), 328.

8 Ewers, *Indian Life on the Missouri,* 12.

9 See A. Doughty and C. Martin, eds., *The Kelsey Papers* (Ottawa: Public Archives of Canada and the Public Record Office of Northern Ireland, 1929).

10 The Naywattame Poets are undoubtedly the Atsina or Gros Ventre and are so identified

by journalists at a relatively early date. See, for example, D. Brymner, ed., *Memoir or Summary Journal of the Expedition of Jacques Repentigny Legardeur de Saint Pierre* (Ottawa: Public Archives Report, 1886), clxi.

11 Tyrrell, *David Thompson's Narrative*, 327.
12 Ibid., 328.
13 Ibid., 329.
14 Ibid., 327.
15 Ibid., 330.
16 Ibid.
17 Ibid.
18 Ibid., 331; 332; 335.
19 G. Flandrau, ed., *The Vérendrye Overland Quest of the Pacific*, Quarterly of the Oregon Historical Society 16, no. 2 (reprint, June 1925), 53.
20 Ibid.
21 Ibid., 53–55.
22 Ibid., 55
23 Ibid.
24 Cpt. Lewis and Cpt. Clark, *History of the Expedition under the Command of Captains Lewis and Clark to the Sources of the Missouri, across the Rocky Mountains, down the Columbia River to the Pacific in 1804–1806*, II (reprint, Toronto: G.N. Morang, n.d.), 120.
25 Brymner, *Expedition of Jacques Repentigny Legardeur de Saint Pierre*, clxi; clxiii.
26 P.A.C., M.G. 18 D5A, Journal of Anthony Henday 1754–1755, 5 September 1754; 11 October 1754.
27 Ibid., 15 May 1755.
28 W.A. Ferris, *Life in the Rocky Mountains 1830–1835* (reprint, Salt Lake City: Rocky Mountain Bookshop, 1940), 76.
29 Ibid.
30 Ibid.
31 P.A.C., M.G. 18 D5B, Journal of Matthew Cocking 1772, 24 August 1772.
32 Ibid., 4 November 1772.
33 Ibid.
34 Tyrrell, *David Thompson's Narrative*, 330.
35 P.A.C. M.G. 18 D5B, Cocking, 14 and 15 December 1772.
36 Tyrrell, *David Thompson's Narrative*, 336.
37 Ibid., 337.
38 Ibid., 338.
39 Ibid.
40 Ibid., 348.
41 Lewis and Clark, *History of the Expedition*, II, 116.
42 A.S. Morton, ed., *The Journal of Duncan McGillivray of the North West Company at Fort George on the Saskatchewan, 1794–1795* (Toronto: Macmillan of Canada, 1929), 49.
43 R.G. Thwaites, ed., *Journal of a Voyage up the River Missouri, Performed in 1811, by H.M. Brackenridge* (Cleveland: The Arthur H. Clark Company, 1904), 28.
44 Tyrrell, *David Thompson's Narrative*, 381.
45 R. Cox, *Adventures on the Columbia River including the Narrative of a Residence of Six Years on the Western Side of the Rocky Mountains among Various Tribes of Indians*

Hitherto Unknown: Together with a Journey across the American Continent (New York: J. and J. Harper, 1832), 233.

46 Tyrrell, *David Thompson's Narrative*, 441.

47 Ibid., 381.

48 P.A.C., M.G. 19 A13, A. Henry's Journey, Lake Superior to the Pacific Ocean, 1799–1816, 1,006.

49 P.A.C. IM49, Hudson's Bay Company Papers – Edmonton Post Journal, James Bird, 15 November 1812.

50 Tyrrell, *David Thompson's Narrative*, 549.

51 Ibid.

52 Cox, *Adventures on the Columbia River,* 118.

53 Ibid., 121.

54 Ibid., 233.

55 P.S. Odgen, *Traits of American-Indian Life and Character by a Fur Trader* (London: Smith, Elder and Company, 1853), 25.

56 A. Ross, *The Fur Hunters of the Far West: A Narrative of Adventures in the Oregon and Rocky Mountains,* I (London: Smith, Elder and Company, 1855), 255.

57 A broad discussion of Indian influence on pricing, the type and quality of goods and general trade strategy is found in A.J. Ray, "Fur Trade History as an Aspect of Native History," in *One Century Later,* edited by I. Getty and D. Smith (Vancouver: University of British Columbia Press, 1978).

58 P.A.C., M.G. 19 A13, Henry's Journey, 1,008.

59 Tyrrell, *David Thompson's Narrative,* 30.

60 Ewers, *Indian Life on the Upper Missouri,* 12.

61 Ibid.

62 P.A.C., M.G. 18 D5A, Henday, 20 September 1754.

63 Ewers, *Indian Life on the Upper Missouri,* 12–13. In the tradition of Weasel Tail, the Blackfoot stole the first horses they ever owned. Ewers and other scholars suggest, however, that horses were acquired through trade.

64 W.K. Lamb, ed., *Gabriel Franchère, Journal of a Voyage on the North West Coast of North America during the Years 1811, 1812, 1813 and 1814,* The Champlain Society, vol. 45 (Toronto, 1969), 150–151.

65 P.A.C. M.G. 18 D5B, Henday, 15 May 1755.

66 E. Umfreville, *The Present State of Hudson's Bay* (facsimile reprint, with an introduction by W.S. Wallace, Toronto: The Ryerson Press, 1929), 31–32; 31.

67 P.A.C., M.G. 18 D5B, Cocking, 4 November 1772.

68 Ibid.

69 G. Williams, ed., *Andrew Graham's Observations on Hudson's Bay, 1767–1791,* The Hudson's Bay Record Society, vol. 27 (London, 1969), 257.

70 Ibid.

71 Tyrrell, *David Thompson's Narrative,* 335.

72 P.A.C., M.G. 18 D5A, Henday, 20 September 1754.

73 P.A.C., M.G. 18 D5B, Cocking, 7 October 1772; J. Bain, ed., *Travels and Adventures in Canada and the Indian Territories between the Years 1760 and 1776 by Alexander Henry Fur Trader* (Toronto: G.H. Morang and Company, 1908), 281.

74 E.E. Rich, ed., *Cumberland House Journals and Inland Journal 1775–1779,* The Hudson's Bay Record Society, 1st ser., vol. 14 (London, 1951), 50.

75 J. Franklin, *Narrative of a Journey to the Shores of the Polar Sea in the Years 1819, 1820, 1821 and* 1822 (facsimile reprint, Edmonton: M.G. Hurtig Ltd., 1951), 50.
76 P.A.C., M.G. 18 D5A, Henday, 15 May 1755.

CHAPTER 2

1 A.S. Morton, *A History of the Canadian West to 1870–1871* (Toronto and New York: Thomas Nelson and Sons, Ltd., 1939), 13.
2 Ray, *Indians in the Fur Trade,* 28.
3 Ibid., 31–35.
4 H.A. Dempsey, *Big Bear* (Vancouver, Toronto: Douglas and McIntyre, 1984). Chapter 2 contains an excellent description of the Plains Cree seasonal cycle.
5 Ibid., 36–37.
6 Doughty and Martin, *The Kelsey Papers,* 13.
7 Tyrrell, *David Thompson's Narrative,* 329.
8 L.J. Burpee, ed., *Journals and Letters of Pierre Gaultier de Varennes De La Vérendrye and His Sons,* The Champlain Society, vol. 16 (Toronto, 1927), 485.
9 Patterson, *The Canadian Indian,* 93.
10 Ibid.
11 Tyrrell, *David Thompson's Narrative,* 330.
12 P.A.C., M.G. 18 D5A, Henday, 17 May 1755.
13 P.A.C., M.G. 18 D5B, Cocking, 19 September 1772.
14 Ibid., 4 November 1772.
15 Bain, *Travels and Adventures in Canada,* 295.
16 Ibid., 300.
17 See: J.B. Tyrrell, *Journals of Samuel Hearne and Philip Turnor,* The Champlain Society, vol. 21 (Toronto, 1934), 103; and Rich, *Cumberland House Journals, 1775–1779,* 355.
18 P.A.C., M.G. 19 B4, Sketch of the Fur Trade of Canada, W. McGillivray, 1809, 16; see also Ray, *Indians in the Fur Trade,* 130.
19 Tyrrell, *David Thompson's Narrative,* 320.
20 E.E. Rich, ed., *Cumberland House Journals and Inland Journal 1779–1782,* The Hudson's Bay Record Society, 2nd ser., vol. 15 (London, 1952), 345.
21 Ibid., 134 (see also Ray, *Indians in the Fur Trade,* 132–133, for a discussion that relates to the Assiniboine); P.A.C., Hudson's Bay Company Papers – Cumberland House Post Journal, Reel IM38, 26 January 1786.
22 P.A.C., Hudson's Bay Company Papers – Buckingham House Post Journal, Reel IM18, 17 January 1793; P.A.C., Hudson's Bay Company Papers – Fort Ellice Post Journal, Reel IM51, 3 March 1794; A.S. Morton, ed., *The Journal of Duncan McGillivray of the North West Company* (Toronto: Macmillan of Canada, 1929), 49; 55.
23 Morton, *Journal of Duncan McGillivray,* 77.
24 P.A.C., Hudson's Bay Company Papers – Carlton House Post Journal, Reel IM19, 2 May 1797.
25 Morton, *Journal of Duncan McGillivray,* 77. "Canadian" refers to fur traders based in Montreal who came west in the 1760s challenging the HBC monopoly. The dominant Canadian company was the North West Company.
26 Ibid.
27 Ibid., 54; 31.

28 P.A.C., Hudson's Bay Company Papers – Setting River Post Journal, Reel IM131, 8 January 1799.

29 Morton, *Journal of Duncan McGillivray*, 77.

30 A.M. Johnson, ed., *Saskatchewan Journals and Correspondence 1795–1802*, Hudson's Bay Record Society, vol. 26 (London, 1967), 6.

31 Ibid., 4.

32 Ibid., 19.

33 P.A.C., Hudson's Bay Company Papers – Setting River Post Journal, Reel IM131, 8 January 1799.

34 P.A.C., M.G. 19 A13, Henry's Journey, 765.

35 O. Lewis, *The Effects of White Contact upon Blackfoot Culture with Special Reference to the Role of the Fur Trade* (New York: J.J. Augustin, 1942), 14.

36 Morton, *Journal of Duncan McGillivray*, 47. For other discussions of motivation in the fur trade that include more than the standard economic interpretation, see: S. Krech, *The Subarctic Fur Trade: Native Social and Economic Adaptations* (Vancouver: University of British Columbia Press, 1984); D. Francis and T. Morantz, *Partners in Fur* (Montreal: McGill-Queens University Press, 1983); C. Martin, *Keepers of the Game* (Los Angeles: University of California Press, 1978).

CHAPTER 3

1 P.A.C., Hudson's Bay Company Papers – Manchester House Post Journal, Reel IM73, 9 June 1787; 31 July 1787; 24 August 1787; 9 June 1787.

2 Ibid., 24 August 1787.

3 Ibid., 28 January 1792.

4 P.A.C., Hudson's Bay Company Papers – Hudson House Post Journal, Reel IM63, 17 September 1782.

5 Johnson, *Saskatchewan Journals*, 285.

6 See: P.A.C., Hudson's Bay Company Papers – Manchester House Post Journal, Reel IM73, 26 April 1788; and P.A.C., Hudson's Bay Company Papers – South Branch House Post Journal, Reel IM143, 24 July 1788.

7 Morton, *Journal of Duncan McGillivray*, 62.

8 P.A.C., Hudson's Bay Company Papers – Buckingham House Post Journal, Reel IM18, 22 October 1793.

9 Morton, *Journal of Duncan McGillivray*, 62.

10 P.A.C., Hudson's Bay Company Papers – Buckingham House Post Journal, Reel IM18, 22 October 1793.

11 Morton, *Journal of Duncan McGillivray*, 63.

12 P.A.C., Hudson's Bay Company Papers – South Branch House Post Journal, Reel IM144, October 1793.

13 P.A.C., M.G. 19 A13, Henry's Journey, 1176.

14 P.A.C., Hudson's Bay Company Papers – Buckingham House Post Journal, Reel IM18, 22 October 1793.

15 Ibid.

16 Morton, *Journal of Duncan McGillivray*, 63.

17 Umfreville, *Present State of Hudson's Bay*, 102.

18 P.A.C., Hudson's Bay Company Papers – Carlton House Post Journal, Reel IM19, 2 May 1797.

19 Morton, *Journal of Duncan McGillivray*, 63.

20 Ibid., 14.

21 Johnson, *Saskatchewan Journals*, 75.

22 P.A.C., Hudson's Bay Company Papers – Cumberland House Post Journal, Reel IM39, 9 July 1794.

23 Ibid.

24 W.K. Lamb, ed., *Sixteen Years in the Indian Country, the Journal of Daniel William Harmon, 1800–1816* (Toronto: Macmillan of Canada, 1957), 97; Morton, *Journal of Duncan McGillivray*, 63; P.A.C., Hudson's Bay Company Papers – Cumberland House Post Journal, Reel IM39, 9 July 1794.

25 Morton, *Journal of Duncan McGillivray*, 35, 39.

26 P.A.C., Hudson's Bay Company Papers – Nippoewin House Post Journal, Reel IM102, 7 January 1795.

27 Morton, *Journal of Duncan McGillivray*, 55.

28 Ibid., 27.

29 Ibid., 69.

30 Johnson, *Saskatchewan Journals*, 294.

31 P.A.C., Hudson's Bay Company Papers – Island House Post Journal, Reel IM65, 7 October 1800.

32 Lamb, *Sixteen Years in the Indian Country*, 51.

33 Ibid., 79.

34 P.A.C., Hudson's Bay Company Papers – Edmonton Post Journal, Reel IM49, 25 August 1806.

35 Ibid., 22 September 1806.

36 Lamb, *Sixteen Years in the Indian Country*, 100.

37 P.A.C., MG. 19 A13, Henry's Journey, 795.

38 Johnson, *Saskatchewan Journals*, 297.

39 R.G. Thwaites, ed., *Travels in the Interior of America 1809, 1810, and 1811 by John Bradbury* (Cleveland: The Arthur H. Clark Company, 1904), 225.

40 D. Mackay, *The Honourable Company* (Toronto: McClelland and Stewart Ltd., 1966), 129–130.

41 P.A.C., M.G. 19 A13, Henry's Journey, 744.

CHAPTER 4

1 Mandelbaum, *Plains Cree*, 169–171.

2 Burpee, *La Vérendrye and His Sons*, 44.

3 Ibid., 59.

4 Ibid., 481.

5 Ibid.

6 Flandrau, *Vérendrye Overland Quest*, 25.

7 Burpee, *La Vérendrye and His Sons*, 117.

8 Flandrau, *Vérendrye Overland Quest*, 27.

9 Morton, *History of the Canadian West*, 177.

10 Ibid.

11 E.E. Rich, *The Fur Trade and the Northwest to 1857* (Toronto: McClelland and Stewart Ltd., 1967), 88.
12 Morton, *History of the Canadian West,* 177.
13 Ibid., 186.
14 Burpee, *La Vérendrye and His Sons,* 222.
15 Ibid.
16 Ibid., 258.
17 Ibid., 280–281.
18 W.R. Wood and T.D. Thiessen, eds., *Early Fur Trade on the Northern Plains* (Norman: University of Oklahoma Press, 1985), 3–6.
19 Burpee, *La Vérendrye and His Sons,* 108; 109.
20 Ibid., 121.
21 See: Tyrrell, *David Thompson's Narrative,* 225, 231; Lewis and Clark, *History of the Expedition,* II, 165.
22 Burpee, *La Vérendrye and His Sons,* 201.
23 Flandrau, *Vérendrye Overland Quest,* 31.
24 P.A.C., M.G. 19 A13, Henry's Journey, 508.
25 Ibid., 3.
26 P.A.C., M.G. 19 C2 No. 5, Journal of John McDonnell 1793–1797, 1.
27 Tyrrell, *David Thompson's Narrative,* 215.
28 P.A.C., M.G. 19 C2 No. 5, Journal of John McDonnell, 1.
29 P.A.C., Hudson's Bay Company Papers – Brandon House Post Journal, Reel IM17, 10 July 1797.
30 Ibid., 25 March 1800.
31 E. James, ed., *A Narrative of Captivity and Adventures of John Tanner during Thirty Years Residence among the Indians in the Interior of North America* (Minneapolis: Ross and Haines Inc., 1956), 70.
32 P.A.C., Hudson's Bay Company Papers – Brandon House Post Journal, Reel IM17, 21 December 1801.
33 Ibid., 2 May 1802 and 28 November 1804.
34 P.A.C., M.G. 19 A13, Henry's Journey, 364.
35 P.A.C., M.G. 19 C2 No. 9, Account of the Missouri Indians, Charles McKenzie, 61.

CHAPTER 5

1 Burpee, *La Vérendrye and His Sons,* 253. See also Wood and Thiessen, *Early Fur Trade on the Northern Plains,* 18–21, for a discussion of whether or not the Mandan visited HBC posts on the Bay.
2 Burpee, *La Vérendrye and His Sons,* 160.
3 Flandrau, *Vérendrye Overland Quest,* 32.
4 Ibid.
5 Ibid., 33; 34, 38.
6 Burpee, *La Vérendrye and His Sons,* 366.
7 Ibid., 367.
8 Ibid., 387.
9 Flandrau, *Vérendrye Overland Quest,* 53; 94.
10 Ewers, *Indian Life on the Upper Missouri,* 16.

11 Flandrau, *Vérendrye Overland Quest,* 34.
12 P.A.C., M.G. 19 A13, Henry's Journey, 502.
13 Lewis and Clark, *History of the Expedition,* II, 220.
14 P.A.C., Hudson's Bay Company Papers – Brandon House Post Journal, Reel IM16, 17 May 1795.
15 Lewis and Clark, *History of the Expedition,* II, 394.
16 See M. Perrin Du Lac, *Travels through the Two Louisianas and among the Savage Nations of the Missouri* (London: Richard Phillips, 1807), 56.
17 P.A.C., M.G. 19 A13, Henry's Journey, 512.
18 Ibid., 559.
19 Lewis and Clark, *History of the Expedition,* II, 183.
20 P.A.C., M.G. 19 A13, Henry's Journey, 550.
21 P.A.C., M.G. 19 C2, No. 9, Charles McKenzie, 35.
22 Ibid., 28.
23 Ibid., 32.
24 Ibid.
25 P.A.C., M.G. 19 A13, Henry's Journey, 587.
26 Ibid.
27 P.A.C., M.G. 19 C2 No. 9, Charles McKenzie, 86; Lewis and Clark, *History of the Expedition,* II, 108.
28 P.A.C., M.G. 19 A13, Henry's Journey, 502. A made beaver (MB) was the standard valuation placed on trade goods and fur by the Company. Goods were measured against the value of one prime beaver pelt. Thus the value of one's hunt or one's fur-post purchase was made up, or calculated, against that standard.
29 Ibid.
30 Lewis and Clark, *History of the Expedition,* II, 367; Ewers, *Indian Life on the Upper Missouri,* 16.
31 Ibid., 23.
32 P.A.C., M.G. 19 A13, Henry's Journey, 502. See also Wood and Thiessen, *Early Fur Trade on the Northern Plains,* 65–66, for other examples.
33 Ibid., 56–58, for information on the type of fur traded out of the villages.
34 P.A.C., Hudson's Bay Company Papers – Brandon House Post Journal, Reel IM16, 17 May 35 1795.
35 Ibid., Reel IM17, 15 December 1796.
36 Lewis and Clark, *History of the Expedition,* II, 195.
37 Innis, *The Fur Trade in Canada,* 264.
38 Ibid.
39 P.A.C., Hudson's Bay Company Papers – Brandon House Post Journal, Reel IM17, 27 February 1805.
40 P.A.C., M.G. 19 C2 No. 9, Charles McKenzie, 11.
41 P.A.C., M.G. 19 A13, Henry's Journey, 593; P.A.C., Hudson's Bay Company Papers – Brandon House Post Journal, Reel IM17, 26 December 1795; 15 December 1817.
42 P.A.C., Hudson's Bay Company Papers – Brandon House Post Journal, Reel IM17, 27 February 1805; 5 February 1796.
43 P.A.C., M.G. 19 C1 Vol. 3, F.A. Laroque, Journal of Missouri River, 7.
44 P.A.C., M.G. 19 A13, Henry's Journey, 442.
45 Ibid., 346.

46 P.A.C., Hudson's Bay Company Papers – Brandon House Post Journal, Reel IM17, 5 August 1796.
47 Lewis and Clark, *History of the Expedition*, II, 221.

CHAPTER 6

1 Tyrrell, *David Thompson's Narrative*, 229. For a contrary interpretation see Wood and Thiessen, *Early Fur Trade on the Northern Plains*, 71–74.
2 Tyrrell, *David Thompson's Narrative*, 229.
3 Lewis and Clark, *History of the Expedition*, II, 220.
4 P.A.C., M.G. 19 A13, Henry's Journey, 458.
5 P.A.C., M.G. 19 C2, No. 9, Charles McKenzie, 61.
6 P.A.C., M.G. 19 A13, Henry's Journey, 561.
7 Lewis and Clark, *History of the Expedition*, II, 183.
8 Ibid, 183–184.
9 Ibid.
10 H.M. Chittenden, *The American Fur Trade of the Far West*, I (Stanford: Academic Reprints, 1954), 126; 159.
11 Thwaites, *John Bradbury*, 102.
12 Ibid., 108.
13 Thwaites, *H.M. Brackenbridge*, 65.
14 R.A. Billington, *Soldier and Brave* (New York, Evanston, and London: Harper and Row, 1963), 6–7.
15 Chittenden, *The American Fur Trade of the Far West*, 329.
16 James, *John Tanner*, 197; 200.
17 P.A.C., M.G. 19 C2 No. 9, Charles McKenzie, 79.
18 P.A.C., M.G. 19, A13, Henry's Journey, 561.
19 Thwaites, *John Bradbury*, 114.
20 P.A.C., M.G. 19 A13, Henry's Journey, 784–785; P.A.C., Hudson's Bay Company Papers – Brandon House Post Journal, Reel IM17, 9 June 1810.
21 P.A.C., Hudson's Bay Company Papers – Brandon House Post Journal, Reel IM17, 18 September 1817.
22 Ibid., 9 November 1817.
23 Ibid.
24 Ibid., 15 December 1817.
25 Ibid.
26 Ibid., 27 January 1818.
27 Ibid., Peter Fidler, 7 March 1818.
28 Ibid., 1 May 1818.
29 Ibid., 28 May 1818.
30 Ibid., 16 November 1818.
31 Ibid., 6 March 1819.
32 P.A.C., Hudson's Bay Company – Fort Dauphin, Reel IM41, 4 June 1819.
33 Ibid., 27 August 1819.
34 J. West, *The Substance of a Journal during a Residence at the Red River Colony, British North America, in the Years 1820–1823* (facsimile reprint, Vancouver: The Alcuin Society, 1967), 77.

35 P.A.C., Hudson's Bay Company Papers – Fort Dauphin, Reel IM41, 3 May 1820.
36 Ibid., 8 March 1821.
37 P.A.C., Hudson's Bay Company Papers – Fort Ellice Post Journal, Reel IM51, 22 December 1822.
38 Ibid., 8 March 1823.
39 P.A.C., Hudson's Bay Company Papers – Fort Pelly Post Journal, Reel IM116, 6 November 1832. Unfortunately there is a gap in the chain of evidence between 1823 and 1831.
40 Ibid, 13 April 1831; April 1831 and 10 June 1831.
41 Ibid., 15 September 1831.
42 R.G Thwaites, ed., *Travels in the Interior of North America by Maximilian, Prince of Wied*, II (Cleveland: The Arthur H. Clark Company, 1905), 382.
43 Ibid., I, 351; see also G. Catlin, *Letters and Notes on the Manners, Customs and Conditions of the North American Indians Written during Eight Years Travel amongst the Wildest Tribes of Indians in North America, 1832–1839* (Piccadilly: G. Catlin, 1841), 191.
44 Thwaites, *Maximilian, Prince of Wied*, I, 391; and III, 65.
45 A.H. Abel, ed., *Chardon's Journal of Fort Clark, 1834–1839* (University of South Dakota: Published under the auspices of the Superintendent, Department of History, 1932), 47.
46 Ibid., 133.
47 Ibid., 165.
48 Ibid., 181.

CHAPTER 7

1 P.A.C., M.G. 19 A13 Henry's Journey, 772. Demographics continue to be an important research area. For references see: H.F. Dobyns, *Native American Demography: A Bibliography* (Bloomington: Indiana University Press, 1976); H.F. Dobyns, *Their Number became Thinned: Native American Population Dynamics in Eastern North America* (Knoxville: University of Tennessee Press, 1983); J. Kay, "The Fur Trade and Native American Population Growth," *Ethnohistory* 31, no. 4 (1984).
2 H.R. Schoolcraft, *Historical and Statistical Information Respecting the History, Condition and Prospects of the Indian Tribes of the United States,* 6 vols. (Philadelphia: Lippincott, Grambo and Company, 1851–1857), III, 556. Estimates are by M. Chauvignerie (1736), Cpt. T. Hutchins (1764) and An Army Officer (1812).
3 Burpee, *La Vérendrye and His Sons,* 256.
4 Tyrrell, *David Thompson's Narrative,* 14; Rich, *Cumberland House Journals, 1779–1782,* 242; Mackenzie, *Voyages from Montreal,* xxxviii; Rich, *Cumberland House Journals, 1779–1782,* 226; 232.
5 Mackenzie, *Voyages from Montreal,* xxlii.
6 Cox, *Adventures on the Columbia River,* 151.
7 Umfreville, *Present State of Hudson's Bay,* 49; and P.A.C., Henry's Journey, 719.
8 P.A.C., Hudson's Bay Company Papers – Fort Pelly Post Journal, Reel IM116, 8 December 1837; 25 January 1837; British Parliamentary Papers, 1858, Report From the Select Committee on the State of the British Possessions in North America which are under the Administration of the Hudson's Bay Company with Minutes of Evidence

(Shannon: Irish University Press, 1969), 43; P.A.C., Hudson's Bay Company Papers – Fort Pelly Post Journal, Reel IM116, 25 January 1837.

9 P.A.C., M.G. 19 B4, Sketch of the Fur Trade of Canada McGillivray 1809, 12–15.
10 P.A.C., M.G. 19 A13, Henry's Journey, 772.
11 British Parliamentary Papers, 1858, 367.
12 P.A.C., M.G. 19 A13, Henry's Journey, 772.
13 Mandelbaum, *Plains Cree*, 189.
14 Schoolcraft, *Historical and Statistical Information*, III, 593.
15 Catlin, *Letters and Notes*, I, 67.
16 Thwaites, *Maximilian, Prince of Wied*, II, 14.
17 Schoolcraft, *Historical and Statistical Information*, III, 611.
18 Major W.F. Butler, *The Great Lone Land: A Narrative of Travel and Adventure in the North West of America* (London: S. Law, Marston and Rivington, 1872), 385.
19 D. Jenness, *The Indians of Canada* (Ottawa: Publications of the National Musuem of Canada, 1960), 317.
20 Mandelbaum, *Plains Cree*, 220.
21 Ibid. See also, for an example of a chief in trouble and the dissolution of a band, Dempsey, *Big Bear*, 143–148.
22 Mandelbaum, *Plains Cree*, 166.
23 E. Denig, *Five Indian Tribes of the Upper Missouri* (reprint, Norman: University of Oklahoma Press, 1969), 111.
24 Ibid., 109–111.
25 They did not always choose that course, however. See Dempsey, *Big Bear*, 143–148.
26 Mandelbaum, *Plains Cree*, 220.
27 Ibid., 224; 225; 300 and 221.
28 Ibid., 221; 222; 229.
29 Kane, *Wanderings of an Artist*, 275.
30 Mandelbaum, *Plains Cree*, 299; Catlin, *Letters and Notes*, I, 57; I.M. Spry, *The Papers of the Palliser Expedition 1857–1860*, The Champlain Society, vol. 44 (Toronto, 1968), 13 September 1857.
31 H.E. Driver, *The Indians of North America* (Chicago and London: The University of Chicago Press, 1969), 323; Mandelbaum, *Plains Cree*, 302.
32 Mandelbaum, *Plains Cree*, 231; 221; Lamb, *Sixteen Years in the Indain Country*, 219; Mandelbaum, *Plains Cree*, 222.
33 Mandelbaum, *Plains Cree*, 224; and 226.
34 Lamb, *Sixteen Years in the Indian Country*, 223; Mandelbaum, *Plains Cree*, 231.
35 Mandelbaum, *Plains Cree*, 222; 234; Denig, *Five Indian Tribes of the Upper Missouri*, 112–113.
36 Mandelbaum, *Plains Cree*, 223.
37 Ibid., 276.
38 Ibid., 204.
39 J. McDougall, *Pathfinding on Plain and Prairie: Stirring Scenes of Life in the Canadian North-West* (Toronto: William Briggs, 1898), 70.
40 O. Lewis, *Effects of White Contact upon Blackfoot Culture*, 58.
41 Tyrrell, *David Thompson's Narrative*, 330; 332.
42 Mandelbaum, *Plains Cree*, 195.
43 O. Lewis, *Effects of White Contact upon Blackfoot Culture*, 59. The argument over the

impact of the horse and gun and, indeed, the nature of plains cultural evolution, is extensive. See, among others: G. Arthur, "A Re-Analysis of the Early Historic Plains Indian Bison Drive," in *Bison Procurement and Utilization: A Symposium, edited by L.B. Davis and M. Wilson (Plains Anthropologist*, no. 14, pt. 2 [1978]); F. Eggan, "The Cheyenne and the Arapaho in the Perspective of the Plains Ecology and Society," in *The American Indian: Perspectives for the Study of Social Change* (Chicago: Aldine Publishing Company, 1966); A. Fisher, "The Algonquion Plains?" *Anthropologica*, 10 (1968): 7–19; B. Mishkin, *Rank and Warfare among the Plains Indians* (Seattle and London: University of Washington Press, 1940); S. Oliver, *Ecology and Cultural Continuity as Contributing Factors in the Social Organization of the Plains Indians* (Berkeley: University of California Press, 1962); C.H. Wilson, "An Inquiry into the Nature of Plains Indian Cultural Development," *American Anthropologist*, 65 (1963): 35–369; C. Wissler, "Diffusion of Culture in the Plains of North America," II, *Proceedings of the Fifteenth International Congress of Americanists* (Quebec, 1906).

44 Jenness, *Indians of Canada*, 256.
45 Lamb, *Sixteen Years in the Indian Country*, 223. For an excellent example of the control of individuals for the sake of existing political-military alliance, see Dempsey, *Big Bear*, 34.
46 Lamb, *Sixteen Years in the Indian Country*, 223.
47 Kane, *Wanderings of an Artist*, 280.
48 J. Macoun, *Manitoba and the Great North West* (Guelph: The World Publishing Company, 1882), 555.
49 Denig, *Five Indian Tribes of the Upper Missouri*, 112.
50 Ibid., 111.
51 Ibid., 99.
52 D.I. Bushnell, *Burials of the Algonquian, Siouan and Caddoan Tribes West of the Mississippi*, Publications of the Bureau of American Ethnology, bulletin no. 83 (Washington, D.C.: Smithsonian Institution, 1927), 6.
53 Mandelbaum, *Plains Cree*, 197.
54 Wissler, "Diffusion of Culture on the Plains of North America," II, 39; M. Barbeau, "The Origin of Floral and Other Designs among the Canadian and Neighboring Indians," *Proceedings of the 23rd International Congress of Americanists* (New York, 1928), 204.

CHAPTER 8

1 P.A.C., Hudson's Bay Company Papers – Edmonton Post Journal, Reel IM49, 20 December 1807.
2 P.A.C., M.G. 19 A13, Henry's Journey, 909.
3 Ibid., 911.
4 Ibid., 918.
5 Ibid., 1,008.
6 Ibid.
7 Ibid., 1,146; 1,116.
8 Ibid.
9 Ibid., 1,118.
10 P.A.C., Hudson's Bay Company Papers – Edmonton Post Journal, Reel IM49, 30 April 1816.

11 P.A.C., M.G. 19 A13, Henry's Journey, 1128.
12 H.A. Dempsey, *A Blackfoot Winter Count* (Calgary: Glenbow Foundation, 1965), 6.
13 P.A.C., Hudson's Bay Company Papers – Edmonton Post Journal, Reel IM49, 11 October 1815.
14 Ibid., 9 December 1815.
15 Ibid., 11 October 1815.
16 P.A.C., Hudson's Bay Company Papers – Carlton House Post Journal, Reel IM19, 3 May 1816.
17 Ibid., 13 December 1816.
18 Ibid., 29 April 1817.
19 Ibid., 22 September 1818.
20 Ibid., 29 September 1818.
21 Ibid., 5 March 1819.
22 P.A.C. Hudson's Bay Company Papers – Edmonton Post Journal, Reel IM49, 19 April 1819.
23 P.A.C., Hudson's Bay Company Papers – Carlton House Post Journal, Reel IM19, 13 December 1816; P.A.C., Hudson's Bay Company Papers – Edmonton Post Journal, Reel IM49, 10 February 1819.
24 Dempsey, *Blackfoot Winter Count*, 7; P.A.C., Hudson's Bay Company Papers – Edmonton Post Journal, Reel IM49, 5 March 1820.
25 P.A.C., Hudson's Bay Company Papers – Carlton House Post Journal, Reel IM19, 30 June 1820.
26 Ibid., 10 July 1820.
27 Ibid., 17 August 1820.
28 Ibid., 24 August 1821; P.A.C., Hudson's Bay Company Papers – Edmonton Post Journal, Reel IM49, 21 April 1822 and 26 February 1823.
29 P.A.C., Hudson's Bay Company Papers – Bow River Expedition, Reel IM20, 3 November 1822.
30 P.A.C., Hudson's Bay Company Papers – Edmonton Post Journal, Reel IM49, 19 April, 1823 and 30 March 1824.
31 Ibid., 15 October 1823.
32 Ibid., 23 April 1824.
33 Dempsey, *Blackfoot Winter Count*, 7.
34 P.A.C., Hudson's Bay Company Papers – Edmonton Post Journal, Reel IM49, 29 October 1825.
35 Dempsey, *Blackfoot Winter Count*, 7.
36 P.A.C., Hudson's Bay Company Papers – Edmonton Post Journal, Reel IM49, 5 December 1825.
37 Ibid., Reel IM50, 4 September 1826.
38 Ibid., 10 November 1826 and 7 November 1826.
39 Ibid., 27 February 1827; 14 March 1827.
40 Ibid., 20 March 1827; 28 March 1827.
41 Ibid., 25 March 1827; 27 March 1827.
42 Ibid., 28 March 1827; 30 March 1827.
43 Ibid., 10 July 1827 and 20 July 1827.
44 Ibid., 7 April 1828.
45 Ibid., 22 March 1828.

46 P.A.C., Hudson's Bay Company Papers – Carlton House Post Journal, Reel IM19, 3 August 1828.

47 Ibid., 17 August 1828.

48 P.A.C., Hudson's Bay Company Papers – Edmonton Post Journal, Reel IM50, 17 October 1827; 4 February 1828; 21 April 1828 (for further details of negotiations see, Dempsey, *Big Bear,* 13-15).

49 P.A.C., Hudson' Bay Company Papers – Edmonton Post Journal, Reel IM50, February 1828, 12 March 1828 and 8 October 1828.

50 Dempsey, *Blackfoot Winter Count,* 8.

51 P.A.C., Hudson's Bay Company Papers – Fort Pitt Post Journal, Reel IM119, 3 August 1830; P.A.C., Hudson's Bay Company Papers – Fort Pitt Post Journal, Reel IM117, 4 September 1830.

52 P.A.C., Hudson's Bay Company Papers – Fort Pitt Post Journal, Reel IM119, 5 August 1830.

53 Ibid., 16 April 1831.

54 Ibid., 14 April 1831

55 Ibid., 4 November 1831.

56 Ibid., 20 March 1832.

57 P.A.C., Hudson's Bay Company Papers – Edmonton Post Journal, Reel IM50, 2 September 1832 and 25 October 1832.

58 P.A.C., Hudson's Company Papers – London Inward Correspondence from Governors of the HBC Territories, Reel 195, George Simspon, 10 August 1824.

59 P.A.C., Hudson's Bay Company Papers – Governor Simpson, Official Reports to the Governor and Committee 1826-1827, Reel 3M44, 25 July 1827.

60 Ibid., 1829-1832, Reel 3M45, 18 July 1831.

61 O. Lewis, *Effects of White Contact upon Blackfoot Culture,* 24.

62 Thwaites, *Maximilian, Prince of Wied,* I, 380.

63 O. Lewis, *Effects of White Contact upon Blackfoot Culture,* 29. See also, for a more accurate account, P.A.C., Hudson's Bay Company Papers – District Fur Returns 1821-1892, Reels IM812-813, Buffalo return figures for the years 1832-1843.

64 P.A.C., Hudson's Bay Company Papers – Governor Simpson, Official Reports to the Governor and Committee 1832-1839, Reel 3M45 21 July 1834.

65 Ibid.

66 Thwaites, *Maximilian, Prince of Wied,* II, 158.

67 W. Lewis and P.C. Phillips, eds., *The Journal of John Work* (Toronto: The Arthur H. Clark Company, 1923), 128.

68 Ibid.

69 Ferris, *Life in the Rocky Mountains, 1830-1835,* 117.

70 P.A.C., Hudson's Bay Company Papers – Edmonton Post Journal, Reel IM50, 30 August 1832.

71 Ferris, *Life in the Rocky Mountains,* 255.

72 Catlin, *Letters and Notes,* I, 22.

73 Thwaites, *Maximilian, Prince of Wied,* II, 146.

74 P.A.C., Hudson's Bay Company Papers – Fort Pelly Post Journal, Reel IM117, 11 November 1833.

75 P.A.C., Hudson's Bay Company Papers – Edmonton Post Journal, Reel IM50, 4 August 1828.

76 Ibid., 30 August 1832 and 2 November 1823.

77 Ibid., 8 December 1833.

78 P.A.C., Hudson's Bay Company Papers – Bow Fort Post Journal, Reel IM16, 17 December 1833.

79 P.A.C., Hudson's Bay Company Papers – Edmonton Post Journal, Reel IM50, 22 December 1834.

80 P.A.C., Hudson's Bay Company Papers – Bow Fort Post Journal, Reel IM16, 10 March 1833.

81 P.A.C., Hudson's Bay Company Papers – Carlton House Post Journal, Reel IM19, 19 July 1833; and P.A.C., Hudson's Bay Company Papers – Edmonton House Post Journal., Reel IM50, 11 July 1832.

82 P.A.C., Hudson's Bay Company Papers – Edmonton House Post Journal, Reel IM50, 17 July 1833; 29 July 1833.

83 Ibid., 19 February 1834.

84 Ibid., 2 March 1834.

85 P.A.C., Hudson's Bay Company Papers – Carlton House Post Journal, Reel IM19, 5 March 1834.

86 P.A.C., Hudson's Bay Company Papers – Edmonton Post Journal, Reel IM50, 9 April 1834.

87 P.A.C., Hudson's Bay Company Papers – Carlton House Post Journal, Reel IMl9, 15 September 1834.

88 P.A.C., Hudson's Bay Company Papers – Fort Pelly Post Journal, Reel IM117, 10 May 1835.

89 P.A.C., Hudson's Bay Company Papers – Carlton House Post Journal, Reel IM19, 14 December 1835 and 2 May 1835.

90 Ibid., 21 June 1836; 18 August 1836; 15 April 1837.

91 Schoolcraft, *Historical and Statistical Information,* II, 258.

92 P.A.C., Hudson's Bay Company Papers – Carlton House Post Journal, Reel IM19, 15 May 1839.

93 Abel, *Chardon's Journal at Fort Clark,* 167 and 178.

94 Denig, *Five Indian Tribes of the Upper Missouri,* 89-90.

95 Mishkin, *Rank and Warfare among the Plains Indians,* 60.

96 Denig, *Five Indian Tribes of the Upper Missouri,* 91.

97 H.M. Chittenden and A.T. Richardson, *Father De Smet's Life and Travels among the North American Indians* (New York: Francis Harper, 1905), 573.

98 Dempsey, *Blackfoot Winter Count,* 11.

99 Chittenden and Richardson, *Father De Smet's Life and Travels,* 524.

100 Ibid., 519.

101 Ibid., 574; and C. Larpenteur, *Forty Years a Fur Trader on the Upper Missouri* (reprint, Chicago: R.R. Donnelley and Sons Company, 1933), 225.

102 Kane, *Wanderings of an Artist,* 304-305.

103 Dempsey, *Blackfoot Winter Count,* 12.

104 Chittenden and Richardson, *Father De Smet's Life and Travels,* 948.

CHAPTER 9

1 J. McDougall, *In the Days of the Red River Rebellion* (Toronto: William Briggs, 1911),

161; H.Y. Hind, *Narrative of the Canadian Red River Exploring Expedition of 1857 and of the Assiniboine and Saskatchewan Expedition of 1858*, II (London: Longman, Green, Longman and Roberts, 1860), 103; F.G. Roe, *The North American Buffalo – A Critical Study of the Species in its Wild State* (Toronto: University of Toronto Press, 1951), 604.

2 Tyrrell, *David Thompson's Narrative*, 142.; J. McDougall, *Forest, Lake and Prairie* (Toronto: William Briggs, 1910), 76; Mgr. Taché, Bishop of St. Boniface, *Sketch of the North-West of America* (Montreal: John Lovell, 1870), 110.

3 Denig, *Five Indian Tribes of the Upper Missouri*, 23 (the Cree also held that the Methodist removal from the Plains of the Iron Stone, a monument to Old Man Buffalo, precipitated this crisis; for details, see Dempsey, *Big Bear*, 37); Hind, *Narrative of the Canadian Red River Exploring Expedition*, II, 311.

4 P.A.C., Hudson's Bay Company Papers – District Fur Returns 1821–1892, Reel IM812–813, Buffalo return figures 1821–1860.

5 Chittenden and Richardson, *Father De Smet's Life and Travels*, 948.

6 Ibid.

7 Viscount Milton and W.B. Cheadle, *The North West Passage by Land – Being the Narrative of an Expedition from the Atlantic to the Pacific* (facsimile reprint, Toronto: Coles Publishing Company, 1970), 37.

8 G.M. Dawson, "Sketches of the Past and Present Condition of the Indians of Canada," reprint from *Canadian Naturalist* 9, no. 3 (1923): 17.

9 I. Cowie, *The Company of Adventurers: A Narrative of Seven Years in the Service of the Hudson's Bay Company during 1867–1874* (Toronto: William Briggs, 1913), 187.

10 Dawson, "Sketches of the Past and Present," 17.

11 Spry, *Papers of the Palliser Expedition*, 145; McDougall, *Forest, Lake and Prairie*, 86.

12 P.A.C., M.G. 21 A13, Henry's Journey, Lake Superior to the Pacific Oceans 1799–1816, 364; J. West, *The Substance of a Journal during a Residence at the Red River Colony, British North America, in the Years 1820–1823* (Vancouver: The Alcuin Society, 1967), 140; G.M. Grant, *Ocean to Ocean – Sanford Fleming's Expedition through Canada in 1872* (facsimile reprint, Toronto: Coles Publishing Company, 1970), 122.

13 P.A.C., Hudson's Bay Company Papers – Carlton House Post Journal, Reel IM19, 26 April 1817.

14 J. McLean, *Notes of Twenty-five Years Service in the Hudson's Bay Territory* (London: Richard Bentley, 1849), 302; see also Dempsey, *Big Bear*, 54–55, for details of a famous clash between G. Dumont and Big Bear in which Cree territorial claims and first rights to the buffalo are advanced.

15 Hind, *Narrative of the Canadian Red River Exploring Expedition*, II, 99; 360; 625.

16 Ibid., 360.

17 Ibid.

18 Ibid.

19 Ibid., 625.

20 Milton and Cheadle, *The North-West Passage by Land*, 66.

21 Cowie, *Company of Adventurers*, 301.

22 Hind, *Narrative of the Canadian Red River Exploring Expedition*, I, 145.

23 Denig, *Five Indian Tribes of the Upper Missouri*, 109.

24 Spry, *Papers of the Palliser Expedition*, 37.

25 H.J. Moberly, *When Fur Was King* (London and Toronto: J.M. Dent and Sons Ltd., 1929), 32.

26 P.A.C., Hudson's Bay Company Papers – Edmonton Post Journal, Reel IM50, 3 December 1854.
27 Ibid., 29 September 1855.
28 Ibid., 25 October 1855.
29 Ibid., 21 March 1856.
30 Spry, *Papers of the Palliser Expedition,* 142; P.A.C., Hudson's Bay Company Papers – Edmonton Post Journal, Reel IM50, 2 September 1857; 13 September 1857; 6 September 1857; 7 September 1857; 27 October 1857.
31 Kane, *Wanderings of an Artist,* 54.
32 Milton and Cheadle, *The North-West Passage by Land,* 163.
33 H.A. Boller, *Among the Indians – Eight Years in the Far West 1858–1866* (Chicago: R.R. Donnelley and Sons, 1959), 39.
34 Larpenteur, *Forty Years a Fur Trader on the Upper Missouri,* 292.
35 P.A.C., Hudson's Bay Company Papers – Edmonton Post Journal, Reel IM50, 28 March 1861.
36 Ibid., 26 January 1862.
37 Ibid., 8 March 1862.
38 Ibid., 7 December 1862; 8 December 1862; 9 December 1862; 10 December 1862.
39 Ibid., 8 March 1862.
40 Ibid., 18 February 1863.
41 Dempsey, *Blackfoot Winter Count,* 13.
42 Larpenteur, *Forty Years a Fur Trader,* 287.
43 Dempsey, *Blackfoot Winter Count,* 14.
44 P.A.C., Hudson's Bay Company Papers –Edmonton Post Journal, Reel IM50, 17 March 1863.
45 J. McDougall, *Saddle, Sled and Snowshoe* (Toronto: The Ryerson Press, n.d.), 107.
46 P.A.C., Hudson's Bay Company Papers – Edmonton Post Journal, Reel IM50, 2 January 1864.
47 Ibid., 8 March 1864.
48 Ibid., 5 April 1864.
49 McDougall, *Saddle, Sled and Snowshoe,* 238.
50 P.A.C., Hudson's Bay Company Papers – Edmonton Post Journal, Reel IM50, 18 February 1865.
51 Ibid., 29 May 1865.
52 Ibid., 24 March 1865; 28 March 1865; 17 June 1865.
53 Ibid., 3 February 1865.
54 Mandelbaum, *Plains Cree,* 167.
55 Cowie, *Company of Adventurers,* 302.
56 Ibid.
57 Ibid., 304.
58 P.A.C., Hudson's Bay Company Papers – Edmonton Post Journal, Reel IM50, 3 April 1869.
59 McDougall, *Days of the Red River Rebellion,* 50.
60 P.A.C., Hudson's Bay Company Papers – Edmonton Post Journal, Reel IM50, 29 June 1869.
61 McDougall, *Days of the Red River Rebellion,* 60.
62 Ibid., 119.

63 Ibid., 121; 130.
64 A. Johnston, *The Battle at Belly River: Stories of the Last Great Indian Battle* (Lethbridge: Historical Society of Alberta, 1966), 4.
65 Ibid., 11.
66 Ibid., 5.
67 Ibid.
68 Ibid., 9.
69 Ibid., 3.
70 Ibid., 8.
71 Ibid.
72 McDougall, *Days of the Red River Rebellion*, 203.
73 Johnston, *Battle at Belly River*, 8.
74 Butler, *Great Lone Land*, 217.
75 Dawson, *Sketches of the Past and Present*, 17.
76 Ibid.

CONCLUSION

1 J. Mooney, "The Ghost Dance Religion and the Sioux Outbreak of 1890," in *American Bureau of Ethnology, Annual Report for 1892–1893*(1896): 634.

Index